Common Parenting Issues

Common Parenting Issues

Handouts for Professionals Working with Children & Families

Cathy Bétoin

Speechmark

www.speechmark.net

DEDICATION
For Pierre, Joshua, Tomas and Daniel and also for Mum and Dad, Meriel, Peter and Rowan.

ACKNOWLEDGEMENTS
This collection of leaflets was born from experience, both professional and personal, and the author's thanks extend to all those who have shared in the learning that is crystallised here. Notable among these are my family and friends who have shared the experience of parenting through some challenging times, and also my clients and work colleagues from past settings and currently from Morecambe Bay Primary Care Trust.

Published by
Speechmark Publishing Ltd, 70 Alston Drive, Bradwell Abbey, Milton Keynes MK13 9HG
Tel: +44 (0) 1908 326944   Fax: +44 (0) 1908 326960
www.speechmark.net

© Cathy Bétoin, 2005
Reprinted 2006, 2008, 2010

002-5261/Printed in the United Kingdom by CMP (UK) Ltd

British Library Cataloguing in Publication Data
Bétoin, Cathy
    Common parenting issues : handouts for professionals working with children and families. –
    (A Speechmark photocopiable resource)
    1. Child psychology   2. Adolescent psychology   3. Parenting
    I. Title
    155.4

ISBN: 978 0 86388 533 4

Contents

Preface

These information leaflets are not intended to be definitive statements about the right way to parent children or solve difficulties.

Parenting is a complex business. The reality for many parents is that we manage, or sometimes just muddle along, doing the best we can with the many different responsibilities that we have. When we encounter problems of various sorts with one or more children, the principal need is often to step back from the general day-to-day routine in order to *think* constructively about what has been or is happening. Dealing with difficulties commonly involves putting ourselves in our children's shoes, talking with others, trying things out and exercising kindness and patience with our child, and ourselves, while things move on. What 'works' at one time, may work less well at another time.

What is critically important is that when things appear to be 'working' between a child and his or her parents or carers, we commonly notice that the child feels cared for, safe with and accepted and supported by the parent. And the parent feels accepted and supported by others and rewarded by the experience of being a parent.

These leaflets are intended to be a stimulus to the process of stepping back and thinking. They can be used when a few ideas are what is needed. For example as:

▷ individual leaflets for parents with a specific concern
▷ a group of leaflets to prompt discussion of different ways of coping
   with difficulties
▷ part of a structured parent coaching/support group
▷ part of professional training for work with children
▷ a general information source in any location used by parents.

It is never too late to have a better relationship with a child!

Cathy Bétoin
November 2004

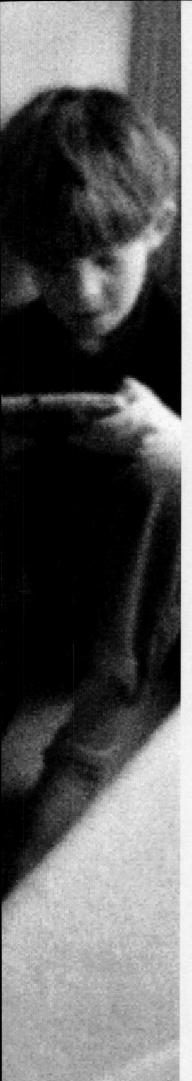

Introduction

The idea for this leaflet pack arose from my experience as a practising clinical psychologist supporting a case load of families with very mixed needs. Many of the families wanted ideas or information and I found myself struggling to find a resource that fitted the bill. I wanted to have some low cost attractive information leaflets on a range of subjects that I could use flexibly with families and health visitors which were not simply scrappy photocopies hastily put together from books. There didn't seem to be such a resource available, so the idea was born!

Common Parenting Issues comprises a series of masters for professional-looking leaflets to support your work with children and families. Covering the range of issues encountered by parents of children aged 0–16 years, the leaflets provide clearly written guidance on how to help children with some of the common problems encountered in family life. They are suitable for families in your surgery, family centre, community mental health team, school, nursery, social work, psychology or psychiatry department. They can be used to support self-help as well as on-going therapeutic work.

Please use the CD-Rom to print a photocopy master for the leaflets that you require. Each of the 51 leaflets comprises two pages and can be printed or photocopied back to back on an A4 sheet and then folded for your leaflet rack or personal resource pack.

I wish you all the best in your work.

Cathy Bétoin

Index of leaflets for professionals and parents

Parents are the most important adults in a child's life. Small changes made by adults in their behaviour towards their children can make a huge difference to their happiness and well-being.

The leaflets in this pack are intended to share simple ideas of the ways in which parents can help their children. They can be used by parents and professionals, carers or volunteers to support a range of situations or ways of working.

If you would like a copy of any of the information leaflets listed overleaf, please contact the following local person who can send you a copy.

_____

Ways the leaflets for parents can be used

These information leaflets are not intended to be definitive statements about the right way to parent children or solve difficulties.

Parenting is a complex business. The reality for many parents is that we manage, or sometimes just muddle along, doing the best we can to juggle the many different responsibilities that we have. When we encounter difficulties of various sorts with one or more children, due to unhappiness or other matters, the principal need is often to step back from the general day to day routine in order to *think* constructively about what has been or is happening. Dealing with difficulties commonly involves putting ourselves in our children's shoes, talking with others, trying things out and generally offering kindness and patience for the child and ourselves, until things move on. What 'works' at one time, may work less well at another time.

What is critically important is that when things appear to be 'working' between a child and his or her carers, we commonly notice that the child feels cared for, safe with, accepted and supported by the parent. And the parent feels accepted and supported by others and rewarded by the experience of parenting.

So these leaflets can be used to support the stepping back process. They may be useful when a few ideas are what are needed. For example:

➤ As individual leaflets for parents with a specific concern
➤ As a group of leaflets to prompt discussion of different ways of coping with difficulties
➤ As part of a structured parent coaching/support group
➤ As part of professional training for work with children
➤ As a general information source in any location used by parents.

It's never too late to have a better relationship with a child!

If you would like to buy the book and CD-Rom of copy masters, *Common Parenting Issues*, please contact Speechmark Publishing Ltd, **www.speechmark.net**.

Welcome to our Child Development Service

1

If you are wondering whether your child has a learning difficulty or emotional difficulties, or if you are sure that this is the case, this may be a very difficult time for you. Perhaps you and others are coping with strong feelings of your own about this situation. You may also be becoming familiar with a world of professionals and places that you didn't know existed.

Professionals and parents realise that the experience can be overwhelming. This leaflet has been written with the help of parents who have been along a similar path. We hope it will give you some ideas of what to expect and some sense of how we feel we can support you.

What are appropriate activities and targets?

When children have difficulties of any sort, it is vital to identify some fun activities which will help your child to make progress, and some small achievable targets to work towards. Clarity about these appropriate activities and targets will help everyone to work together to help you to help your child.

Professionals can help you understand the activities, but to make best progress much of the work to help your child will inevitably take place in your own home environment. It can be helpful to see yourself and your extended family as your child's main 'therapists', and to accept that in the long run you are your child's main source of self-esteem and self-confidence. *Remember though, parents and carers often need help and support with their own needs to be able to help their child effectively.*

What should I do if my child has special educational needs?

One of the things that the staff in our Child Development Service can help you to decide is whether your child has special educational needs. Most children with delays, disabilities or emotional difficulties attend mainstream schools. Other children are happier in more specialist provision. These decisions don't usually have to be made straight away, but it will be useful to discuss the options with you.

A final note

Parents and extended family are often very distressed to learn that their child may have difficulties. They can experience a whole range of emotions, including shock, denial, guilt, anger, sadness and depression. Adjusting can take some considerable time. But accepting the reality of the difficulties is usually an important step towards being able to take responsibility for helping your child.

Professionals in our Child Development Service will try to support you through this process. This might include putting you in touch with other local parents who have experienced similar things to yourself.

Useful local contacts include: _____

How can I get help?

If you and a professional who knows your child agree that there is a reason to be concerned about your child's development, you can be referred to the Child Development Service. Your child and family will have the opportunity to meet with one or perhaps several different professionals, all of whom have specialist knowledge of different aspects of child development. They will talk with you, and observe your child and will work with you on some detailed developmental assessments. Your knowledge of your child is essential to these professionals if they are to be able to make an accurate assessment. Remember the service is confidential so please share with them everything you know and have observed.

What is a developmental assessment?

The aim of a developmental assessment is to identify the areas in which your child is having difficulties, as well as their areas of strength. It is important to know this so that we can understand how to best help your child.

To be helpful to a child, it is necessary to think about their *current* skills and understanding, and about their *current developmental age* not about their real age. When a child is having difficulties, we often need to think about their needs as if they were a younger child. But, as children develop rapidly our assessment process is always ongoing.

What can I do?

Unfortunately, professionals cannot just sort your child's problems out for you. As it is you that can spend most time with your child *we see it as our role to help you to help your child*. We can, for example, help you to understand more about development and about your child's difficulties. We will be able to give you support as well as advice and recommendations about the sorts of activities that will help your child to progress.

First questions first

What is a developmental delay or disability, and what are emotional difficulties?

If a child has a developmental delay or disability, it means he or she is developing more slowly in certain areas than other children. If your child has emotional difficulties he or she may not currently be feeling very secure in their relationships, or confident in themself. A child can have just one or both types of difficulties.

Will I be given a diagnosis?

It is not always possible to give a clear diagnosis, although parents often find diagnosis quite helpful.

Is it my fault?

NO! Many parents who have contact with the Child Development Service worry that others will think they are to blame for their child's difficulties. It is not helpful to suggest that parents are to blame. Childhood difficulties are surprisingly common, and their causes are not yet always fully understood. Parents need adequate information and support themselves to be able to do their job.

Will my child ever catch up?

WE OFTEN DON'T KNOW. Young children's development is very varied. In general, the more significant the delay, the more unlikely it is that your child will catch up completely with other children. This does not mean that your child cannot have a full and interesting life. But he or she is likely to need more support from you.

Can I make a difference?

YES! Although it is not helpful to blame parents, parents do have key responsibilities. It is important for parents to feel confident about their own central role in caring for their child. This includes taking active steps to support the child with the full range of skills they will need as they grow up. The younger the child, the easier it is to help start this process.

Carrying out your own developmental assessment: 0–5 years

Professionals who work with young children use a variety of detailed assessments to understand your child's current skills and needs.

This leaflet is an attempt to give *you* an idea of the some of the different areas of skill that are commonly looked at. Remember that many children have uneven development. They usually have strengths in some areas and weaknesses in others. However, if your child's development is delayed more than three months in the first year, or more than six months in the second year in any area it is very important to seek advice promptly.

The table in this leaflet should give you some ideas of what usually happens in child development. To use the chart:

i)   Draw a line on the chart to show your child's actual age,

ii) Work out what your child is currently able to do in each area,

iii) Work out what skills your child may need more support with.

iv) Provide more opportunities to help your child to practice and develop existing skills,

v)   *Don't* be tempted to rush your child on before he or she is ready.

What is a multidisciplinary assessment?

In a multidisciplinary assessment, different specialists contribute their expertise to help understand your child's current skills and needs more fully.

⋗ A *paediatrician* has expertise in the medical aspects of child health, including your child's physical development and emotional health.

⋗ A *clinical psychologist* has expertise in supporting your child's psychological development in the context of the needs and events in the wider family.

⋗ A *health visitor* has a background in nursing and will support you with your child's developmental needs at home.

⋗ A *speech therapist* has expertise in the development of your child's speech and communication skills.

⋗ A *physiotherapist* has expertise in the development of your child's gross motor, movement and mobility skills

⋗ An *occupational therapist* has expertise in the development of fine motor skills, and in helping children to manage the skills of daily living.

⋗ A *teacher* will wish to support your child in learning those study skills play skills and group skills, necessary for school learning. A *nursery nurse* often supports teachers

⋗ An *educational psychologist* has a role in helping decide what your child will need to help them cope well in their school placement.

⋗ A *child psychiatrist* has expertise in medicine and prescription drugs as well as in mental health.

⋗ A *social worker* has expertise in the benefits and support services available to support you and your family in the local district.

Developmental Assessment: From 0–5 years   *This chart will give you some ideas about what usually happens in child development.*

Age	Sensory control and gross motor skills	Attention	Eye and hand	Cognitive development and play skills	Social interaction and emotional literacy	Hearing and speech	Behaviour and emotional development
0–6 months	Head control; Back control; Happy to go down; Likes feeding, baths; Likes movement; Dribbling ending; Works against gravity: rolls, sits, crawls, stands	Can tolerate some noise, movement, without upset; High distractibility with moments of stillness and focussed attention (1 min); Turns to familiar voices; Can track with gaze; Looks for dropped object; Predicts cause and effect	Brief grasp reflex; Hand to mouth action; Watches hands, feet; Catches hanging item; Passes objects hand to hand; Picks up small object with thumb & finger; Finger feeds	Finding own body in space, kicking, pushing, pulling etc; Bangs together; Likes one or two simple books; Constant exploration; Returns to interesting places eg cupboards	Likes being handled; Early brief smiling; Makes eye contact; Watches faces, smiles and laughs; Likes lap games, singing, peekaboo; Prefers familiar faces; Follows familiar people; Likes to be carried	Stills to hear voice; First sounds, babble; Listens to music, song; Makes 'conversation'; Responds to name; Waves bye bye; Lots of babble; Ma-ma, Da-da etc	Sensory systems still maturing; Startles easily to sound, movement; Needs gentle care, and adult to mesh behaviour to fit infants needs; Likes to keep close to carers; Has transitional comforter; Sleep patterns settling
6–12 months	(see above)						
12–18 months	Becoming active; More stability in walking with heels, climbing steps; Running	Focuses on game or object for 3–5 min or more but focus will shift rapidly (NB: Cannot easily follow adult focus, adult must attend to child's focus to support integration of looking, listening, understanding)	Likes mark making; Puts things in and out of containers; Throws a ball	Likes simple books; Imitates observed behaviours, with real objects eg cups, spoons	Looks to others face for cues for behaviour; Wants to stay close to attachment figures	Indicates wants by pointing; Understands 'Where's?', 'No!' and simple phrases; First clear words	Upset by separation; Likes to do own thing; Needs *routines*, rests, lots of help/supervision; No unusual behaviours, eg flapping
18–24 months	Jumping; Rough and tumble; Balance developing; Can correct wobbles		Feeds self with spoon; Copies lines; Builds tower of two bricks; Helps put toys away if supported	Pretends actions with cars, dolls; Not just lining up; Can find or match some identical objects	Follows a point and points; Shows things to others; Sustained turn-taking if supported in 1:1; Observant of emotions	Joins in simple songs; Starts to link 2–3 words together; 50 words	Will eat at table; Social skills developing in play with supportive and firm others; Some toileting readiness
2–3 years	Variety of activity needed; Increasing stability in kicking, balancing on one leg; Pedalling tricycle; Walks upstairs one leg at a time; Will calm if hurt	Often sustains attention for 10 min or more on self-selected exploratory activities; Starting to be willing to briefly stop own activity to be guided in focus of attention; Needs quiet times and warnings; Easily distracted by noise	Copies circle, crosses; First recognisable figures; Likes drawing, dough, inset puzzles, easy building; Likes sand and water; Starts to use scissors; Takes off clothing	Sequence of actions in pretend play; Uses objects as if they were something else (symbolically); Invents new ideas in imaginative play; Likes dressing up; Games show variety	Likes to watch or play closely by or in parallel with peers; Co-operates with brief group/adult directed activity; Plays easily with one supportive peer; Loves helping; Separates if feels safe; A few words for emotions	Some use of pronouns; Three word phrases; Asks basic questions; First references to past and future; Listens to short story; Understands longer sentences; Talk to self; Expanded vocabulary	Seeks independence *and* closeness; Experiences much frustration; Testing limits; Needs routines, rests, kindness and firmness; Will walk holding hands, follow simple instruction; Tantrums can be settled; First thinking of others
3–4 years	Likes physical play; Need often higher in boys than in girls; Sustained pedalling; Hops, balances on a line; Catches large ball; Doesn't bump into others	Likes sustained problem-solving play, 15–20 mins; Still needs calm and prefers to choose own activity; More easily tunes into adult focus; Sits still and attends to 10 min adult-led/ group activity; Still has to stop and look to listen	Likes construction; Puts on shoes; Undoes buttons; Likes simple puzzles; Can thread beads; Can build a bridge; Can draw a person	Builds 3D objects; Colours-in pictures; Plays lotto, matching games, dominoes; Makes stories in sand, water play, small world; Dresses up and takes roles in games	Runs errands; Starts to develop more interest in peer play; Able to mesh own play actions with range of peers; Begins to listen to and understand other person's views and feelings with empathy	Asks more questions; Longer clear speech; Start of true turn taking in conversation; Listens carefully; Shares feelings about past and future events; Language not strange	More co-operative; Follows social rules and complies with requests; Waits turn; Learning to share toys and objects with others; Restrains self to seek approval; Gets tired; Usually dry and clean in day
4–5 years	Climbs downstairs in adult manner; Can walk a distance; Two-wheel bicycle	Sustains attention in busy setting; Occasionally able to listen and modify own behaviour without stopping; Follows instructions to group	Can dress self, fold clothes; Can cut out shapes; Can count bricks	Increased complexity in play sequences, construction or drawing	Likes play with others; Negotiates with others; Understands public conventions; Beginning to express feelings in words	Can describe a short sequence of events; Talks confidently with range of people; Wide vocabulary	Can manage in a group; Can be given small responsibilities; Takes care of younger children; First coping with losing

3. Using a developmental assessment to support early intervention with your child

If you or others are concerned about your young child's development, it is important to carry out a developmental assessment. This leaflet will give you some ideas about how to use a developmental chart to understand your child's difficulties. Remember children can have learning difficulties or they can have emotional difficulties. Sometimes they can have both. Difficulties can be mild, or more severe, and sometimes the difficulties lie in the circumstances around the child. This leaflet will help you to start thinking about what you can do to help your child.

Remember, children develop at different rates, but if there is a difficulty, it is early home-based intervention that is most likely to be effective in helping your child. You have a very important role to play – but don't forget that your needs are important too.

Some points to remember

▲ When assessing your child's difficulties with a developmental chart, it is probably better to under-estimate your child's skills than to over-estimate them. It is probably better to support your child unnecessarily than not to help them when they needed it!

▲ There is *reason to be concerned* about your child's development if your child shows delays in any area of:
  – More than three months in the first year
  – More than six months in the second year
  – More than nine months in the third year.

▲ Definite diagnoses are very difficult to give when your child is young. It is therefore important to continue to observe your child closely, and carry out tests if necessary, but it is also important to get on with the business of offering your child the right sort of help as early as possible.

▲ It is not helpful to blame yourself or others for your child's difficulties. You are not to blame, but you can now make a difference. Parents are potentially a child's best therapists.

▲ Acceptance of the reality of your child's difficulties takes time but is an essential step in the process of working out how to take responsibility for best helping your child. Don't be surprised if this takes time.

▲ Whatever the explanation for your child's difficulties, your child will *need* a positive relationship with you and others. It is important to work out how to connect with this child.

▲ Professionals are there to support and advise you. This leaflet has only given examples. Keep talking to others if you are still worried.

An Introduction to development

The interesting thing about child development is that children usually develop skills in a predictable order. If children have delays in development in any given area, we can still expect them to make progress – and usually in the same order as any other child.

This is very helpful when thinking about how to help your child. It means that we must first find out what your child can do now, as well as how confident he or she feels with you and others, and then we must work out how to help your child to learn the skills that he or she is finding more difficult than other children. The question that you must ask yourself is, 'What is my child's current developmental age, and how can I give my child more support and opportunities in order to learn the next key skills?'

A note on diagnosis

When parents begin to become concerned about their child's development, they often feel that that they must have a diagnosis to explain what is happening. This is understandable, but in practice, when a child is very young professionals often don't know exactly why a child is having difficulties. They may agree with you, however, that *there is good reason to be concerned.* Unfortunately, they may not be able to be more specific than this. However, if there is good reason to be concerned, there is also good reason to take steps to help your child in a proactive way – as soon as possible, without waiting for the certainty of a specific label.

A note on early intervention

All the research evidence now shows that if a child begins to show developmental difficulties in the first five years of life, it is a good idea to take active steps straight away to work out to help the child. *It is not a good idea to simply wait and see.* Children often do not 'just grow out of' their early difficulties.

Early diagnosis is very difficult. However the following examples may give you some ideas.

If your child has *delays in gross motor and fine motor skills including eye and hand co-ordination*, or if he or she was very irritable, or unusually placid, as a baby he or she may be having difficulty with muscle tone or with co-ordinating sensory inputs. Your child may have a **sensory integration difficulty,** something called **cerebral palsy** or perhaps **dyspraxia.** Your child will need lots of patience from you and practice with sensory, movement and co-ordination skills.

If your child has *delays in speech and language,* your child is having difficulty making sense of sounds. He or she may have some **hearing loss** or **a speech and language disorder.** Your child is likely to need lots of opportunities to practise making sense of sounds and language.

If your child has *delays in social interaction, play and language,* your child is probably having difficulty making sense of the wider social world, not just language. Your child may have a mild or a more pronounced **autistic spectrum disorder.** He or she will need lots of patience from you and carefully planned help to learn about the social world of people, language and emotions.

If your child is *very active or has a short attention span,* your child is probably finding it difficult to sustain concentration on non-physical activities. Your child may need **time to mature,** have **Attention Deficit Hyperactivity Disorder (ADHD)** or be experiencing a lot of **anxiety.** For now he or she clearly needs lots of patience, exercise, and positive supervision and support from adults.

If your child has a lot of *challenging behaviour* with you, it is possible that other delays mean that he or she experiences a lot of **confusion or frustration,** or perhaps he or she doesn't feel totally confident or secure in your presence. Your child may have an **attachment disorder** and may need your help and determination to develop a more positive parent–child relationship.

If your child has *delays in several areas,* he or she may have a **general learning difficulty.** He or she will need extra support from you and others for some time with a full range of skills.

Carrying out your own developmental assessment: 6–16 years

The professionals who work with children use a variety of detailed assessments to understand children's current skills and needs.

This leaflet attempts to give *you* an idea of the some of the different areas that you can consider. It is important to realise that many children have uneven development. They usually have strengths in some areas and weaknesses in others. Boys commonly develop language and social skills more slowly than girls. However, if your child appears to be having difficulties in any area, it is very important to seek advice promptly.

The chart overleaf will give you some ideas about what usually happens when children are supported. To use it:

i) Draw a line on the chart to show your child's actual age,

ii) Work out what your child is currently *able* to do in each area,

iii) Work out what skills your child may need more support with

iv) Provide more opportunities to help him or her to practice and develop existing skills

v) *Don't* be tempted to criticise or rush your child on before he or she is ready.

Some points to remember

⚠ Children are all different. They have strengths and weaknesses. Whatever your child's strengths and weaknesses, their self-esteem is the most crucial factor that will affect their long-term happiness and well-being.

⚠ Self-esteem comes from knowing that important people like you as you are, believe that you are a great sort of person to have around and are ready to make time to listen to you. Self-confidence comes from feeling that important others admire what you can do and the feeling that you can achieve the things that you want to achieve.

⚠ Poor self-esteem comes from feeling that important people don't like you as you are, don't like having you around and don't have time to listen to you. Poor self-confidence comes from feeling that important others don't think you are any good, and the feeling that you can never achieve what you want to achieve.

⚠ Parents have the most important role to play in their child's self-esteem. Children have an inbuilt need to seek their parent's positive attention and affection, to impress them and please them. This is because from the youngest age, they are totally dependent on the parent's care. If the child's confidence and self-esteem becomes damaged. The child's feelings for the parents can become very mixed up.

⚠ To help improve your child's self-esteem and self-confidence you must recognise the strong latent desire of every child to please and impress both parents, and trust themselves, and you must acknowledge or structure your time with your child to make it possible for them to begin to do this. It may take time to work out how, but it is essential if you wish to help.

Developmental Assessment: From 6–16 years   This chart will give you some ideas about themes in the development of children

Age	Behaviour and emotional development	Sensory control and gross motor skills	Attention and memory	Eye and hand	Cognitive Development	Social interaction	Speech/language, reading and writing
6–8 years	Appears relaxed in self Sleeps readily Mainly confident about school work Talks positively about own abilities Participates in clubs Enjoys time with parents Helpful around house	Clear handedness Walks, runs, jumps with stability Can move in many different ways Can ride a bike Can run and kick a ball Can swim a width	Can sustain attention on a self-selected task for 30 min Can listen to instructions in a group setting Can complete work without close supervision in a class environment Remembers items for school	Holds pencil correctly Makes most letter shapes smoothly Can look and draw Can put together small pieces of construction games	Can invent an extended story with small world or role play Can plan/find items needed for a task Can count to 100 and complete simple sums with four operations	Likes playing with other children Has one or more friends with whom he plays often at school and at home Seeks out affectionate contact with others Cares for a pet	Speaks clearly with a range of people Describe an event Can spell a range of simple words Can read simple texts Can write a short account of an event
9–11 years	Appears relaxed in self Can be trusted Mainly confident about school work Talks positively about own abilities and friends Participates in clubs Still enjoys some time with parents Helpful	Can catch and move with a ball in small team games Can do a handstand against a wall Can swim a length No weight problems	Is interested in particular hobbies and shows sustained interest in them Can listen and think critically about what is being heard Takes pride in completing work to high standard	Can thread a needle Can write clearly and neatly Likes complex construction activities with much detail	Can reason through a problem Can plan and complete a task, eg making a meal Can invent own creative ideas in play Can use maths in every day life	Friends very important Becoming aware of being an older child in school Interested in viewpoints Likes responsibilities Cautious curiosity in other sex	Can describe a complicated situation, taking into account the listener Likes reading more complex texts Can write a detailed account of an event with reasonably accurate spelling and punctuation
12–14 years	Seek independence *and* closeness Unpredictable, unsure Many anxieties Underlying themes still essentially positive Needs parents around but not interfering Helps out if encouraged Boys timing different from girls	Manages sustained exercise easily, eg long walks, team games Perfecting skills Eats regularly and with balanced diet Self-conscious	Takes an interest in a hobby/non-school activity and is committed to finding out more Remembers and completes school work and homework tasks Takes share in home tasks	Can look and draw with some detail May play instrument Likes making things if encouraged Advanced computer games	Becoming interested in justice/injustice Enjoys film/story/drama and inventing stories Enjoys problem-solving	Friends and sense of being like others very important Maintains respectful relationships with key adults outside the family Curious about sex, drugs, alcohol	Continues reading Can articulate own point of view in speech and in writing Thoughtful but critical of adults
15–16 years	After rebellious phase Moves to becoming more relaxed in self Ideas about future plans Generally confident in own abilities and hopeful about the future	Maintains regular exercise and involvement in sport or physical activity Aware of healthy eating	Takes part in clubs or hobbies Completes school work and homework tasks Shows critical understanding	Completes fine motor tasks with accuracy and awareness Can word-process a letter	Coping with a range of subjects Takes responsibility for preparing for exams	Girlfriends/boyfriends Participating in range of groups/clubs Relates well to one or two adults outside family	Can write a clear letter for a job application Can describe own interests and strengths in speech/writing

Looking at your family history

Understanding your child's needs

If you think that your child has a difficulty, it is always useful to spend some time thinking carefully about the wider circumstances affecting your family. A careful family history can help you to begin to think about whether your child has learning difficulties or emotional difficulties, or a bit of both.

Overleaf you will find a family tree. Try to fill in as much detail as you can. You will probably find it useful to do this with a professional or an adult who knows you well who can encourage you to think carefully. As you are filling it in, remind yourself that the aim of an assessment is not to seek to blame anyone but to understand better. It is only by understanding things differently that change can be allowed to happen.

Some useful questions to ask yourself

Start by filling in as much detail as possible on the chart overleaf.

▲ Were there any difficulties during the pregnancy of this child or at the time of this child's birth? Was it a planned pregnancy?

▲ What was the child's infancy like? Were there any unusual features? (You might like to look at a developmental chart to help you think this one through?)

▲ When did you first notice your child had difficulties, or when did they get worse? Was anything else happening at the time?

▲ Has anybody else in the extended family ever had learning difficulties or mental health problems?

▲ Who is/are the primary carer(s) for this child? Who has been, and currently is, supporting the primary carer? How have his/her needs been being met? Who else has cared for the child?

▲ Have there been any other major life events or stresses in the child's life, or in the primary carer's lives, since the child's birth? This includes house moves, separations, illnesses, births of siblings, deaths in the family, accidents, arguments, aggression and violence in the family, low incomes, multiple demands and/or work stresses etc.

▲ What sort of parenting did the primary carers have? Were there any important or distressing experiences in the life of the parents when *they* were children, which continue to play an important role?

▲ Now, try to pull your ideas together. Can you see any links? Which bits of evidence do you think are important? What would help now?

Your child's family tree

Fill in as much detail as you can. Put a ring around the people who currently live with your child.

Any major stresses that may have affected you and your child _____

Any major stressful relationships that still affect you and your child _____

Important aunts/uncles

Paternal grandfather

Paternal grandmother

Maternal grandmother

Maternal grandmother

Important aunts/uncles

Other partner

Other partner

Father's work/interests

Father's friends/support

Mother's work/interests

Mother's friends/support

Referred child

Sibling 1

Sibling 1

Sibling 2

Child's school _____

Child's friends _____

Parenting children from birth to 16 years

The relationship between children and adults has changed a lot in the last decades. Many parents often feel confused about what is needed from them. But there is clear psychological research to show that children whatever their age, sex, temperament or skills, need certain things from their parents if they are to grow up to be reasonably confident and happy adults.

If you have a difficult relationship with your child at present, there are things that you can do to make a difference.

This leaflet will look at parenting in more depth and make suggestions of how you might help yourself and your child.

Some points to remember

Every child is different. Some children are more challenging than others.

⚠ All children need to know that their parents basically like and love them unconditionally, as a unique and special person in their own right. Without this, the relationship will always be filled with tension and conflict.

⚠ The most important thing to keep intact with a child is a relationship that has some mutually positive feelings. *Parents have more responsibility for the quality of this relationship than the child.*

⚠ Criticism will not change a child's behaviour in a positive direction. Support, descriptive praise, compliments, time and increased maturity can do.

⚠ Children need to be able to move away from their parents and work out what is important to them. They need parents to take a positive but not overinvolved interest in their developing self. As children become adolescents, parents need to try to shift from being 'managers' to 'consultants'.

⚠ Children learn self-discipline gradually. Parents need to be able to be firm but must never forget trust, respect, kindness and affection.

⚠ All parents learn their first lessons about how to be parents from their own parents. It can therefore be useful to take a critical look at what we experienced as a child in relation to our own parents. Which parts of your experience were positive and helpful, and which weren't?

⚠ Your child needs friends. Always make it a priority to support your child in building and sustaining helpful friendships.

⚠ No parent can parent effectively without having their own needs for support met by other adults. Extended families and communities have a vital role in supporting effective parenting.

Elements of effective parenting

Children need different things from their parents at different times. Whether your child is a toddler or a teenager, he or she will sometimes behave like an older child and sometimes like a younger child. These changing needs of the child call on parents to be *flexible and patient*.

But, whatever the age, sex, temperament or abilities of the child there are three key elements in effective parenting. These are:

➤ consistent feelings of warmth and affection from the parent to the child

➤ consistent supervision and age-appropriate rules which help the child to learn self-discipline and respect for others

➤ a readiness to let go of absolute control combined with an attitude of trust in, and respect for, the choices that children make as they work out their own identity.

A parent's main goal is therefore to help their child to gradually but steadily develop the skills that allow him or her to take on more of the responsibilities associated with adulthood. You have a big role to play in your child's feelings of self-esteem and self-confidence.

When difficulties arise in parenting

Young children need affectionate relationships and firm rules, limits and boundaries. Teenagers also need affectionate relationships as well as a readiness on the part of the parent to gradually allow and respect the teenager's desire to exert more independence in their decision-making.

So, *this is critically important*: if your child feels that he or she cannot trust you to provide reliably supportive care, trust and affection, he or she will always struggle to make the transition to mature and self-confident behaviour in adulthood. He or she may remain bound by anxiety, or bound by the need to control what happens. Parents have an important ongoing role in working out how to keep the relationship positive and helpful.

If your relationship with your child is under strain

If your relationship with your child is under serious strain at the moment, it is very likely that your child feels that you do not care for, or believe in his or her capacities. Or perhaps they feel that you are disinterested in or disapproving of the things that are really important to them at this time. This probably brings out the worst in them. You may be caught in a vicious cycle.

You may think that your child should know that you care for them whatever. *But they probably don't.*

You may be feeling so worried or cross about some things that they are doing, that you want them change. You may *want* your child to know you are upset. But this may not be the best way to achieve your goals. Unwittingly, you may be pushing them further along the very course that worries you.

As a parent your main strength lies in your relative maturity and your ability to **step back and think**. As a parent you can:

➤ Be proactive – what steps can *you* take?
➤ Commit to affection for, and respect of, your child's potential.
➤ Take your child's development age into account.
➤ Think carefully about what you want to achieve.
➤ Put first things first – relationships are the priority.
➤ Try to understand your child's view before trying to make your child understand you
➤ Think win–win – how can everyone gain?

Showing your child you care

Children will decide about your feelings for them on the basis of what you do. Your child doesn't need expensive gifts. However, your child does need to hear compliments and trusting encouragement. He or she needs you to take an active interest in things that interest them, as well as feeling they can have time with you on ordinary things. Friendly and affectionate contact: a hug, a back rub or a tickle can all speak volumes.

How stress affects parenting, and how to help yourself

Parenting children is demanding and can be stressful. But sometimes there are other things in the lives of parents that contribute to general levels of tension. It is often when stresses become combined that parents find their patience with their children wears thin. It is in these conditions that parents can find themselves, irritable, exhausted and overwhelmed.

It is important to become actively aware of these other stresses because sometimes we can start to think that it is just our children that are the problem. This can cause damage to our child and to our relationship with them.

This leaflet looks at some of the other issues which can cause stress for parents and will explain how, by helping yourself, you can help your child.

Some points to remember

△ Stresses add up over time. Most people can cope with some stress but start to experience mental health problems including irritability, anxiety and depression when stresses are too much.

△ To be an effective parent it is very important to find ways to manage or bring down your own stress levels so that when you are actually with your children you are able to remain *mostly* calm, patient and affectionate with them.

△ Stress levels can be reduced by learning to say 'No' to things, by practising relaxation, by exercise and by building in breaks and opportunities for fun for yourself *without* your children. Isolation and boredom is one of the biggest stresses on parents. Keep up your own interests and contact with other adults.

△ Sometimes it is important and helpful to find someone to talk with about things that have happened in your life that are still causing you distress and affect how you feel about yourself.

△ Extreme stress on parents during the early years of a child's life can contribute to a child having a temperament that is more challenging to manage. To reduce the levels of conflict between yourself and a temperamentally challenging child it is vital for you as a parent to find ways to reduce your own stress levels.

△ Taking active steps to build a positive and enjoyable relationship with your child will provide the best stress reduction programme in the long run. It is worth persevering!

△ If you are still worried, talk to your GP or health visitor.

The symptoms of stress

The symptoms of stress start to show in our bodies when we have been coping with a great many pressures for a long time. The symptoms include: difficulties getting to sleep or staying asleep; irritability and bad temperedness; tearfulness; bowel troubles; anxiety; depression; increased smoking; drinking or eating; susceptibility to illness and infection including recurrent colds and infections; loss of interest in sex; tiredness; persistent fatigue and exhaustion; and negative thoughts about the self and the future.

The impact of cumulative stress on parenting

When we are experiencing the above symptoms it is difficult to be an effective parent. We have less energy for listening and for being patient and calm. We tend to over-react and shout, or hit out. We may feel so weary that we don't have the energy or interest to organise activities for our children that will keep them out of mischief. If our children have challenging temperaments we may know that we are making things worse and this can make us feel bad about ourselves, guilty and/or very sad.

Things that can contribute to the normal stresses of parenting

➤ Adjusting to the needs of a temperamentally challenging or disabled child.

➤ Moving home

➤ Conflicts or arguments with other members of the family

➤ Different needs of several children or family members

➤ Low incomes

➤ Changing jobs or conflicts at work

➤ Coping alone or not feeling supported

➤ Coping with unresolved feelings about past events

➤ Death, sickness or trauma within the family

The impact of stressed parents on children

Unfortunately children tend to react to stress in their parents with behaviour that is more and more challenging. For example,:

➤ they may learn they have to behave badly in order to get any reaction at all from a stressed, distracted parent;

➤ they may feel they can never do anything right so see no point in trying to be good;

➤ they may copy patterns of dealing with frustration by shouting or hitting out;

➤ they may become withdrawn and reluctant to talk to a parent who always appears angry or critical;

➤ they may settle badly and sleep unsoundly;

➤ they may find it difficult to settle and concentrate;

Coping with stress so as to be able to parent better

It is not always possible to walk away from the causes of stress that we are experiencing. However, if you are aware that the stresses are negatively affecting your parenting there are some positive steps you can take to make a difference:

➤ become aware of the various sources of pressure on you at the moment, notice that many of them are not your child's responsibility;

➤ are there some pressures that you could reduce by saying 'No' to some of your current responsibilities?

➤ identify some people who could support you in various ways by listening, or with some child care.

➤ think of some ways to introduce some calm times into your week – some with your children and some alone

➤ learn and practise the art of relaxation and self-care

➤ work out how to introduce a more positive tone in your relationship with your child/children.

Helpful patterns in healthy families

Being a parent is very difficult. Every parent struggles to offer their child a good experience and every parent has times when they feel overwhelmed and inadequate for the job. Parents often parent as they were parented even though this may not have been a happy experience for them. Becoming a parent is therefore an opportunity to rethink and question your own experiences.

Many people feel the modern world makes parenting more difficult than it has been in the past. There is often a lot less support and, because relationships between children and adults have changed a lot in recent times, parents often feel exhausted and confused about what is needed from them and about how best to help their children.

If you are thinking about your own parenting skills, this leaflet may give you some ideas to consider. Are there steps that you could take to make these patterns more obvious in your own family life?

Speechmark ⓢ ℗ This page may be photocopied for instructional use only. *Common Parenting Issues* © C Bétoin 2005

Some points to remember

▲ Once you have taken the step of having a baby, you become responsible. You are committed to supporting your child's well-being and happiness until it becomes an adult.

▲ Parenting skills are not innate, they have to be learned. Parenting is always hard work and demands effort. It is never too late to rebuild a damaged relationship.

▲ If your family doesn't run in a happy way, it is up to you to take steps to get support and learn some new skills. Like any management skill, running a 'happy-ish family' in a smooth and effective way takes practice and perseverance. No one can do it without help.

▲ One of the most important skills of being a parent involves making time for your own needs and self-care, at the same time as thinking about your children. If other family members can't help you then you may need other support networks.

▲ If you have experienced a lot of trauma and unhappiness in your own childhood, the tasks of parenting are likely to be much more challenging for you. It will help if you can find support to help you to work out how to offer a different experience for your own children. Remember not to be too harsh on yourself if you sometimes find it very difficult.

▲ Some children *are* more difficult to parent than others. They demand more from parent's time, patience and resources. However, challenging children *will* respond to the same sorts of approaches as average children if you are determined.

▲ Wherever possible, children need their mother and their father because mothers and fathers provide different things to a child. If a child's parents are separated, the child has a right to a relationship with both parents. Parents have a joint responsibility to help make this as positive as possible for the child.

▲ If you find parenting challenging, don't worry you are not alone, but it is worth working at!

Speechmark ⓢ ℗ This page may be photocopied for instructional use only. *Common Parenting Issues* © C Bétoin 2005

Helpful patterns in healthy and happy families

Here are some patterns found in an idealised family. Remember when reading this list that there are no ideal families, every family works differently. However, if things are currently difficult, these patterns might give you some ideas of areas or issues to work on.

Authority and attitudes to relationships

⚞ The adults know relationships are difficult and expect to have to work at them

⚞ The adults are basically in charge and support each other

⚞ The adults are ready to respect value and support each child's unique unfolding personality. Each child can be different and special.

⚞ The adults create a basically positive atmosphere. They show kindness and firmness

⚞ The adults listen carefully to the needs, experiences and feelings of others

⚞ The adults believe in their children's capacity to be competent, helpful and thoughtful and actively encourage these qualities

⚞ The adults support the child in developing a full range of skills

⚞ The adults support the child in building helpful friendships and activities

⚞ The adults know the child is learning and therefore allow and forgive mistakes

⚞ The adults consistently notice and appreciate all positive behaviours and progress

Routines and Supervision

⚞ The adults *make time* to keep building and rebuilding a positive relationship with their children

⚞ The adults try to keep *some stability and routines* in the way the household runs

⚞ The adults *plan* to prevent trouble. They do not blame or take sides with at them

⚞ The adults have some clear and reasonably *consistent rules* about behaviour in a range of situations. There are *clear consequences* if rules are broken

⚞ The adults *supervise* their children. They know how their children are spending their time, who they are with and how they are behaving

⚞ The adults *are able to say 'No' and to insist* on certain things even when this makes the child feel cross or frustrated

⚞ The adults insist that all members of the household *play a part* in the day-to-day tasks in running the home. The older the child, the more that is expected of them

⚞ The adults respect the child's right to more responsibilities and decision making as he or she gets older. As the child's skills develop, they are *ready to trust* the child and gradually to let go.

Support for adult needs

⚞ The adults get their main support from other adults and not from their children.

⚞ The adults are involved in other activities and groups outside the home. They are committed to developing their own skills.

What is assertiveness, and how can it help parenting?

Conflicts and disagreements are inevitable in our lives. But people commonly behave in different ways in conflict situations. Some styles of handling conflict such as the aggressive and passive styles are commonly ineffective or make difficulties worse. They are not associated with self-confidence. Effective parenting usually relies on being able to have good skills in assertiveness.

This leaflet looks at the four different styles of handling conflict, known as aggressive, passive, passive-aggressive and assertive.

It explains more about the skills of assertiveness and about situations in which assertive behaviours may be able to help you or your child.

Some points to remember

⚠ The majority of people use some, or all, of the different styles of handling conflict at one time or another. Take time to watch yourself and work out your most common style

⚠ We often react to the styles of handling conflict used by others around us without being aware of it. It can be useful to take time to stand back and work out what is happening in your different relationships with others.

⚠ Using assertiveness skills in our dealings with others takes practice, especially with others who are using other styles! But anyone can learn the skills! It might be useful to go on a course with others

⚠ Assertive people are good at taking responsibility for their own choices and actions

⚠ Assertive people are able to put their own thoughts and feelings and needs into words

⚠ Assertive people are able to listen carefully to others. They are good at negotiating agreements with others which recognise that different people have different needs

⚠ Teaching children assertive behaviour will help them in all areas of their lives. One of the best ways to teach assertive behaviour to your children is to model it yourself

⚠ Children respond well to assertive parents because the parents can be firm but they are also respectful and sensitive

⚠ Living with confident, assertive children and adults can be exhausting! But not as exhausting as living with people who use other styles of handling conflict!

Three unhelpful styles of handling conflicts

The following styles of handling conflict can be seen in any relationship with others. None of these methods are very effective in the long-run. There is evidence that people who rely heavily on any one of these styles often lack confidence inside themselves.

Passive or Permissive

▲ The person/parent tends to/wants to avoid conflict at all costs.

▲ They tend to let things pass or give into unreasonable demands.

▲ Their own needs consequently get overlooked.

▲ The child/other may have too much control and is not experienced in the habit of considering others.

Aggressive or Authoritarian

▲ The person/parent insists on being in control at all times.

▲ They tend to demand things of others in overtly hostile, rude or physically aggressive ways.

▲ The child's/other person's needs are denied or overlooked.

▲ The child/other may be frightened or equally hostile and aggressive in relationships with others.

Passive-aggressive: coercive

▲ The person/parent expresses views or tries to exert control or manipulate others in *indirect* ways such as through subtle sarcasm, put-downs and/or deliberate lack of co-operation.

▲ The person denies importance of their own or others feelings.

▲ The child/other find themselves feeling frustrated, angry, and resentful, and not sure why.

An effective style of handling conflict

People who are reasonably confident tend to have good skills in assertive communication and behaviour. But, most confident people have had to learn these skills. Assertiveness comes with practice!

Assertive: authoritative

▲ The person knows they are responsible for their own choices, behaviours, feelings and thoughts.

▲ The person is able to state their own thoughts, feelings and needs directly and appropriately.

▲ The person listens accurately to the needs and feelings of others.

▲ The person works for agreements which ensure respect for the needs and feelings of all parties.

▲ The child/other feels acknowledged and respected and is more able and likely to behave respectfully in turn.

How to speak assertively to others

▲ Always remain calm.

▲ Prepare yourself carefully – ask yourself what the person cares about and be respectful of this.

▲ Look directly at the person you are speaking to.

▲ Speak firmly and confidently.

▲ State the problem as you see it: 'I am concerned about...'

▲ State your feelings about the problem: 'When *x* happens, I feel ...'

▲ State what you want in a very respectful way.

▲ Listen carefully to the other person (what are their views, feelings, wishes? Can you accommodate in any way?)

▲ Take time out to think, if you need to, and then restate your own position, in a way that indicates that you have heard the other person's needs and concerns.

▲ Firmly *insist* on a solution, but be ready to acknowledge disappointment!

10 Encouraging a secure attachment between you and your child

Research in child development is now clear that one of the most important influences on a young child's development and well-being is the quality of the early *attachments* that they have with their parents.

Children's attachments with their parents are often described as being secure or insecure. A secure attachment between a child and his or her parents seems to help a child's sense of basic safety, and hence their inner and outer feelings self-confidence. Insecure attachments are often associated with patterns of behaviour that are hard to handle. But parents can make changes that will make a difference.

This leaflet looks at 'attachment behaviours' in more depth and explains how you can help improve the quality of your relationship with your child.

Some points to remember

➤ Children develop secure attachments with carers who respond consistently in ways that make them feel better or good inside. Children want to spend more time with adults with whom they have positive and secure attachment experiences.

➤ Adults who develop secure attachments with their children tend to be reasonably calm, patient, positive, encouraging and supportive of their child, responding flexibly to the different needs that they have at different times. These are all skills that can be practised by anyone!

➤ Try to find two lots of 15 minutes or half an hour a day to play with your child by giving your child full attention and letting him or her take the lead.

➤ It is easier to develop a secure attachment with some children than with other children. Irritable babies or babies with disabilities or communication delays are often particularly demanding to care for, as their development is slower and they often seem to give much less back in the early years.

➤ Most adults cannot continue to be patient unless they have reliable and regular breaks for themselves. Other family members and the wider community therefore have an important role to support the primary carers with their task.

➤ Attachment quality is not fixed. If adults begin to change their behaviour towards the child so that the child finds the relationship more enjoyable and helpful, the child will want to begin to approach this adult again.

➤ Do ask for professional advice if you are still worried.

What is attachment behaviour?

Young infants cannot survive without adults who take care of them. They are therefore born with patterns of behaviour that help them to stay close to those who will care for them. If a young infant is hungry or frightened he becomes tense and will cry out. The carer normally hears these cries and comes to help.

By the end of the first year infants have usually learned that when they cry out that there are one or two adults who usually come to help them. These familiar caring figures are their 'attachment figures'. When an infant has learned that these carers usually help them to feel better they are pleased to see them. This shows in all their behaviours. They are happiest when they can stay close. We can say these infants are developing a 'secure attachment'.

Sometimes, however, children have the experience that their key carers do not reliably help them feel better. Maybe the adult is not very confident as a parent, or seems very stressed, tense or rejecting. Maybe the child has been upset by a long separation and is worried the parent might leave again. The child then has confused feelings. He or she wants to come close to the carer but also wants to stay away. The behaviour can seem to be awkward and difficult to understand. We can say that the infant is developing an 'insecure attachment'.

Individual differences in babies

But babies are also different from birth. Some 'easy' infants are quite settled at birth and it is therefore less difficult to have a rewarding experience when looking after them. In these cases secure attachments develop easily.

However, some infants are much more irritable, active and/or unsettled from birth. They demand much more patience and skill from the parent. Without patient willingness from key carers, to help the more challenging infant, insecure attachments can develop more easily. This is where carer support is vitally important.

Children who are securely attached:

- Know they can trust their carers to be supportive and helpful
- Appear self-confident
- Explore the world around them in an active way
- 'Check in' regularly with their attachment figures
- Find relationships with others enjoyable and get on easily with peers and adults
- Are relatively easy to parent and generally enjoy parenting.

Children who are insecurely or anxiously attached:

- Live with a lot more anxiety
- Appear less self-confident and/or not needing of others
- Are not confident that others are reliably there for them
- May be more attention-seeking, demanding or jealous, or controlling
- May be more challenging to parent and may find parenting more challenging and/or stressful
- May have more longstanding mental health difficulties.

The impact of separations or life changes on attachments

Separations and big life changes for young children can be very stressful and need, wherever possible, to be planned carefully. Children need help to:

- Understand what is going to happen and what is happening
- Be reassured that important relationships are not changed
- Have help keeping as many things as normal as possible.

When unavoidable separations or life changes have happened:

Children may need help to:

- Understand what happened
- Understand that the separation or life change was not their fault
- Keep in touch with important relationships
- Have help feeling sad and grieving for changes that have happened and cannot be reversed.

We often choose to believe that events that happen in our everyday lives *cause us* to feel certain things and cause us to behave in certain ways. However, this idea is unhelpful. It suggests that we are helpless victims of circumstance.

We now know that a person's feelings and behaviour are strongly influenced by the thoughts that go through their heads during or after any given incident. Our thoughts represent the things that we learned about ourselves and about the world around us, in our childhood. Unfortunately, sometimes the thoughts that go through our head are understandable in terms of what happened a long time ago, but are unhelpful in terms of what is happening now. Sometimes they are wrong, or out-of-date, and are causing us trouble! Fortunately, these thoughts can change.

This leaflet will help you start thinking about your thoughts in order to work out which thoughts are helpful and which are unhelpful to you in your life and in your relationships with others.

Thinking about thoughts

It is helpful to think of our minds as being capable of three sorts of thinking.

The first sort of thinking happens very fast, and automatically, in response to the trigger events that happen to us. This sort of thinking takes place in our **'emotional brain'**, or our **'inner child'**. The automatic thoughts that go whizzing through our heads when things happen are based on the ideas that we developed about ourselves and others when we were small. It may take time to find out what these ideas were as many of them will have been laid down without speech. Some can be linked with very strong and/or painful emotions.

The second sort of thinking also happens very fast, and automatically, in response to the trigger events that happen to us. This sort of thinking represents the ideas that our parents and other carers had about the world, about us and about our behaviour. It is our **'adapted brain'**, or our **'inner parent'**. As children, we listen to what our parents say about us and about others, and about the world, and because they dominate our world, we can believe that it is all true. As adults, we can often find that their voices or the ideas that they had about the world keep repeating in our head.

The third sort of thinking happens much more slowly and demands much more effort from us. This is the thinking of our **'integrating brain'** or **'mature adult self'**. When we start to use this sort of thinking, we recognise that the first two sorts of thinking may be out-of-date, limiting us or causing us trouble in our current lives.

To use our more mature integrating brain, we have to begin by taking responsibility for understanding and accepting the existence of a full range of our own feelings and behaviour. This includes beginning to take a supportive, curious but critical interest in the ideas that we picked up about ourselves and about the world when we were small. With support, we can learn to be a friend to ourselves and talk to ourselves in more constructive ways.

Try using the chart overleaf to begin thinking about your own thoughts in situations that have been or are causing you trouble. You may find it helpful to do this work with a skilled therapist.

Thinking about thoughts (be more attentive to the negative thoughts which are likely to be more limiting to you).

Trigger event	Fast automatic thoughts My inner child	Fast automatic thoughts My inner parents	Consequences for my behaviour	How others respond to my behaviour	Were the outcomes positive?
	Slow integrating thoughts My mature adult voice … Spotted them! Some automatic thoughts! I can *pause*, think and question. What alternatives could there be?		Consequences for my behaviour	How others respond to my behaviour	Were the outcomes positive?

Finding calm in a challenging world

When we are under stress, we often find that our minds become full of racing, repetitive or negative thoughts about the past, the present and the future. When we examine them closely, we realise that these thoughts are often associated with feelings of anxiety or helplessness or depression. Because our minds are so full, our bodies are tense and we are less open and relaxed in the present moment. Life can feel out of control. Because we are feeling uncomfortable in ourselves, our relationships with others can be affected.

But, there are things that you can do to help yourself, and to help others around you. This leaflet explains how the practice of relaxation and meditation can help you find some peace of mind, and the ability to remain calm during the challenging parts of family and everyday life.

Some points to remember

▷ Change is inevitable. Life will bring happy experiences and less happy experiences. You cannot prevent these things happening to you, or to members of your family. But you can choose how to respond to them.

▷ We can often believe that it is external events that are causing us to feel stressed. Or we may believe that we have no control over our fast reactions to these events and can't manage them. Both of these ideas are incorrect.

▷ Thoughts and feelings need to be taken seriously. They give us insights into the things that really matter to us, and insights into how we have learned to maintain a sense of safety in the world we grew up in. Sometimes we can realise, by tuning in to our thoughts and feelings, that we need more help from others.

▷ Meditation practice teaches those that use it that we can *choose* how we respond to external events or to internal thoughts. It teaches individuals to *take responsibility* for their own responses. By practising the skills of taking care of ourselves, relaxation and concentration on the breath, it is possible to learn to be aware of the fast reactions of our minds and bodies, giving us the option of creating a small *gap*, before responding. Through such practice, we can begin to notice and make way for those thoughts and responses that are most helpful to us and to our relationships with others, and to let go of those that are most unhelpful.

▷ If you are someone who has developed a habit of worrying, try giving yourself a specific but limited time of the day in which to do your worrying – write your worries down if you need to, but try thought-stopping at other times. Remember, to begin to feel calmer, your mind needs a break.

▷ Many people find that joining a meditation, relaxation or yoga classes provides them with helpful support for regular practice.

The cumulative impact of stress and the symptoms

Most children and adults can cope with some stress but start to experience mental health problems when stresses become too much. The symptoms include: difficulties getting to sleep or staying asleep, irritability and bad-temperedness, destructiveness, tearfulness, bowel troubles, anxiety, depression, increased smoking, drinking or eating, susceptibility to illness and infection, including recurrent colds and infections, loss of interest in sex, persistent tiredness, ruminative worrying and negative thoughts about the self or future.

Gaining control of the activity of the mind: taking care of ourselves

Have you noticed how when you are feeling stressed, your mind is frequently preoccupied with unpleasant or negative thoughts of the past or worried thoughts of the future? And have you ever noticed that these negative thoughts can be triggered by the smallest of events and can themselves generate feelings of anxiety, anger, tension, and depression?

To be able to face external stresses with more peace of mind it is essential to realise that the activity of the mind can be controlled. It cannot be controlled by critical bullying of ourselves, but control can be achieved with kindness, firmness and patience. In meditation we learn to become aware of the thoughts that disturb our peace of mind, and then we practice letting go of these thoughts, for a short while. We practise moving our attention from anxious unhelpful thoughts to something neutral or helpful in the present moment, like the breath, or a beautiful object. With practise, an undisciplined, fast reacting, tense mind can be transformed into a more centred, calmer, and relaxed one. We experience improvements in our own well-being and our relationships with others can improve.

Mindfulness, breathing and body scan meditations

Meditation can be an opportunity to practise having a relaxed body and an alert focussed mind. It provides an opportunity to practice being fully aware with concentration on something that exists *in the present moment*.

➤ Choose a relatively quiet place to meditate where you won't be disturbed.

➤ Make yourself comfortable so that you can breathe easily. Sit in a chair with your back well supported, or lie comfortably on the floor.

➤ Take a minute to scan your body and notice if there are any points of tension. Relax them out. Take a deep breath and sigh, let your stomach feel loose.

➤ Now, bring your attention to your breath. Notice the feeling of the breath as it comes in through your nostrils and out through your mouth. Don't try to control it, just watch it.

➤ Gently try to maintain your focus of attention on your breath. You might count slowly from one to three with each breath. Practise staying with a relaxed body and a focussed mind.

➤ You will probably find that you lose concentration and that your attention is interrupted by thoughts of the past or the future. As soon as you can, notice these thoughts (what sort of feelings do they generate in you?), then, for now, *let them go* and return to a focus on the breath. Tell yourself you will deal with them later.

➤ Fifteen minutes of practice of relaxation and breathing on a daily basis will begin to give you the tools for managing a whole variety of stressful circumstances.

Encouraging eye contact: the beginnings of social communication

It is now known that to develop skills in language and social communication, infants have to learn to look at other people's faces and feel comfortable in contact with others. Most children begin to do this from six weeks of age. However, some children seem much less interested in looking at others. Other children are very sensitive and do not appear to enjoy cuddles from an early age. These children are at much higher risk of developing delays in their language and social skills and difficulties in their social relationships.

This leaflet gives you some ideas about how to encourage more eye contact and affectionate contact between you and your young child.

Some points to remember

▲ It is through warm *eye contact* and affectionate contact that children learn about positive relationships with others. It is much easier to learn about a supportive social world if you look carefully at other people's faces, and like cuddles with others. Most infants begin to take an interest in other peoples faces from the age of about six weeks. But in some children these skills take much more time to develop.

▲ By looking carefully at the face of familiar people, infants learn about emotions. They learn to read meanings from facial expressions. Through *imitation* they learn how to change their own face to show others what they are thinking and feeling. By a combination of looking and listening, they also learn how to move their mouth and tongue to make different sorts of sounds.

▲ When infants have learned how to read other people's faces they can look to others to know what to do in new situations that are unfamiliar to them. This is an important skill called 'social referencing'.

▲ When infants don't seem to like eye contact or affectionate contact, it can sometimes be very unrewarding to care for them. Adults may be tempted to give up. *But it is worth persevering.* By making the social world accessible, fun and really interesting for infants, without overwhelming them, we can encourage infants to begin to look more closely at faces, and to enjoy contact with others. This will help the language and communication skills of any infant. But it is particularly important for a child who has delays in social communication.

▲ The drawings inside this leaflet will give you ideas of how to increase these opportunities for your infant.

▲ Do ask for professional advice if you are still worried.

Encouraging eye contact (Illustrations from Beck & Williams (1999), *Ride a Cock Horse*, reproduced with permission from Oxford University Press)

Bouncing and dancing rhymes

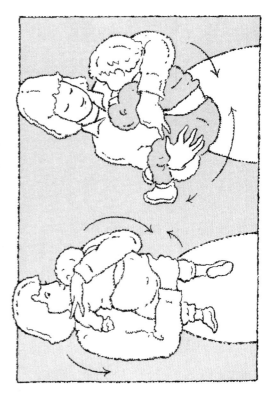

Lullabies and rocking rhymes

Patting and clapping rhymes

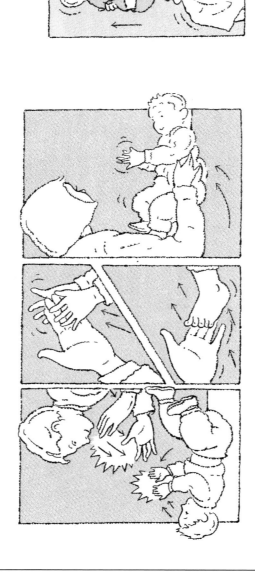

Knee-jogging rhymes

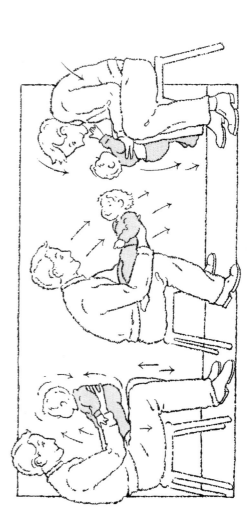

Songs and rhymes to develop joint attention, language and play skills

Joint attention refers to the situation when two people are thinking about the same activity. One of the best ways of helping young children with delays in attention, language and play skills is to use song and rhyme to get them interested in the music of sounds, and the repetition of familiar actions. By repeating songs and rhymes over and over again, and combining them with simple actions, children start to hear familiar sounds and recognise patterns. They begin to anticipate what comes next. This improves their willingness to listen and watch carefully and helps their other language and communication skills

This leaflet will give you ideas of some of the most popular and useful rhymes and songs to use at home with your child.

Some points to remember

➤ It doesn't matter if you think you can't sing. You're not singing for the world, you're singing for your child!

➤ Be as enthusiastic and as expressive as you can – without being overwhelming.

➤ Use rhymes and song whenever you can throughout the day. You can use them during one to one play times with your child but you can also use them during daily routines such as mealtimes, nappy changes, getting dressed.

➤ The more you repeat songs and rhymes, the more familiar they will become to your child and the more he or she will enjoy them

➤ There are some good tape collections of nursery rhymes and songs but many children enjoy adult music as well, including pop and classics such as Mozart and Chopin. These are good for bed-time but don't use them as a substitute for your own singing!

➤ Don't be afraid to invent your own songs, or change the words to songs that you know already. Wherever possible combine your songs and rhymes with gestures and movements. Your child will enjoy being tickled and rocked, and will enjoy joining in with actions to words or anticipating being lifted up or falling down, as in Humpty Dumpty.

➤ Wherever possible try to be on a level with your child when you are singing to encourage them to look at the actions and movements in your face. You want to interest them in faces as much as possible.

➤ Encourage different members of the family to sing with your child.

Developing joint attention, language and play with games, songs and rhymes

Joint attention refers to the situations when two people are thinking about the same thing. Joint attention is very important for the healthy development of children. Young children or children with delays cannot easily join in with adult's thinking. To develop this skill, adults must first be ready to join in with the child.

Basic steps

➤ Make a point of regularly watching and observing carefully what your child is doing – describe aloud what you see.

➤ Repeat your child's sounds and actions; this shows them you are paying attention, and develops their own awareness.

➤ Add a small detail into the play activity your child has chosen

➤ Encourage lots of eye contact

➤ Use excitement, energy and enthusiasm

➤ If you want to, use song.

Good lap games to develop early skills in joint attention

➤ Peek a boo: Where is it? Gone! Here it is! Hello! Where are you?

➤ Nibbling fingers and toes, blowing gently on face or body

➤ Tickling games: ready, steady, go!

➤ General rough and tumble (remember: find ways to gain eye contact)

➤ Blowing bubbles

➤ The Farmer's Horse

➤ Pat-a-Cake

➤ Humpty Dumpty

➤ Row, Row, Row your boat

➤ This Little Piggy went to Market

➤ Round and round the garden

➤ Rock a Bye Baby.

Action Songs that you can adapt

➤ The wheels on the bus go round and round.

➤ Here we go round the mulberry bush (This is the way we brush our hair...)

➤ Heads, shoulders, knees and toes

➤ Where is Andrew? Where is Andrew? Here he is here he is

➤ Hokey Cokey.

Don't Forget the Old favourites!

➤ Baa Baa Black Sheep

➤ Happy Birthday

➤ One Two Three Four Five

➤ Five Currant Buns in a Baker's Shop

➤ Peter Plays with One Hammer, One Hammer

➤ Old Macdonald

➤ Wind the Bobbin up

➤ Ten Green Bottles.

Keep Talking! Make the social world fun!

Children with language and communication delays can often retreat into their own world, which feels familiar and safer. By singing, talking and interacting with your child as much as possible, you will show him that the social world is interesting and understandable. It is worth persevering!

A note on TV addiction and repetitive play

Many children with communication delays enjoy TV and video and very repetitive forms of play. However it is important to remember that during these times your child may be entranced by the television but not mentally active – and therefore not learning as much as they could if they were talking or playing. Too much television restricts language development.

15 Choosing toys and activities to help your child's development

As young children develop, they benefit from a changing range of toys and activities. A few carefully selected toys will give more benefit to your child than lots of toys that are not well-adapted to your child's current stage of development.

If your child has developmental delays of any kind it is particularly important to make available toys that are appropriate to your child's developmental age, not his or her real age. This will help your child to progress more than trying to give them more 'grown up' activities.

The chart in this leaflet will help you to work out the sorts of toys and activities that will best help your child at the moment.

Some points to remember

▲ Children's skills in attention, language and play develop gradually in a step-by-step fashion. Your young child needs different sorts of play opportunities including:
– Time to explore his or her world by himself
– Regular time with adults on a one-to-one basis
– Opportunities to interact with other people.

▲ If your child has delays in attention, language and play skills he or she will be particularly helped by one-to-one play with adults. It is vital to let the child have plenty of experience of taking the lead in these one-to-one sessions. You can add language and ideas.

▲ Your child's interests will change gradually, but children often like to revisit books and toys that they enjoyed at a younger age. Don't discourage this or put your child's interests down.

▲ Try to arrange your home so that your children have a play space that is not too far away from where you are normally busy. This way you can talk to them as you go along. Make your house as 'child-friendly' as you can so that you don't have to keep saying 'No' all the time.

▲ Remember, all young children need their day broken up into short bursts of different sorts of activities. They like to play for a while and then they often need a change of scene such as a walk, a visit to a friend or a trip to a park. Bored children become disruptive and hard to handle.

▲ Don't hesitate to ask for advice from your health visitor, nursery, or at your child development service if you have any concerns.

The Changing Toy Box: From 0–7 years   *Remember it is important to choose toys appropriate for your child's developmental age.*

Age	General features of this age	Outdoor Play	Investigative play	Social Play	Pretend Play	Expressive Play	Books
0–6 months 6–9 months 9–12 months	First steps in gross motor and fine motor control, social interaction, listening and experiments with sounds	Walks out in prams and pushchairs with a chance to see the world Freedom to roam in a safe area	Toys for watching, listening to, grabbing, chewing: mobiles, classical music, songs, rattles, activity centres, containers to be filled	Infant needs plenty of *face to face, eye contact and turn-taking games* with adults, siblings etc Mother and baby groups	Transitional objects, such as a comforter, teddy, doll and/or soft blanket Peep bo, hide and seek	Exploring sound and movement Loves games in which sounds and movements are imitated by others	Soft books or board books with simple pictures or photos of objects, people Limit TV to half an hour
12–18 months 18–24 months	Much movement and activity needing close supervision Lots of single words Gradual emergence of two-word and later three-word combinations	Trolley or buggy to push along, sit on buggy Visits to the park Sand pit with containers, animals, and vehicles	Shape sorters, pulling and pushing toys, pop-up toys, music and sound makers of various kinds Simple inset puzzles First construction	*Plenty of close interaction* with adults/older children very important for emerging language skills Mother and toddler groups	Dolls, teddys or blankets, tea set, toy phone Vehicles of various kinds: cars, tractors, trains, play mat	Thick wax crayons Plenty of paper for scribbling Water play with range of objects Play dough, rolling pin, and cutters	Board books with clear pictures, lift the flap books Nursery rhymes, songs and poems books Limit TV to half an hour
2–4 years	Becomes absorbed in own play Still finds it difficult to shift focus to co-operate with group or with adult Comprehension better, sentence length increasing.	Tricycle to sit on Swing, climbing frame, slide, ball Local walks with dolls in buggy, etc Local visits	Puzzles, bricks, Duplo®, threading beads, train set Sand and water play with characters Musical instruments	Plenty of conversation time with adults, older children Play sessions with peers Play group or nursery	Tea set, train set, cars and garage, farm and animals, zoo and animals, dolls house and people, soft toys, doctor's kit, dressing up items, glove and finger puppets	Pens and paper, stickers Play dough, paint First scissors, magazines to cut out Cooking	Books with simple story line, small amount of text per page, about children doing familiar things Use books to talk about wider world Limit TV to half an hour
5–6 years	Finds it easier to co-operate in group and follow directions for short periods Tells stories, asks lots of questions	Scooter, roller skates Big and small balls Bats and racquets Interesting trips out Longer regular walks	Puzzles with more pieces Lego®, Knex®, Meccano® Start an instrument	Beginnings of social games, eg picture lotto, dominoes, etc Needs peer play	More dressing up clothes Realistic models of dolls, vehicles etc Puppets	Pens and paper, play dough, painting Junk modelling Cut and stick	Wider ranging material, factual, fantasy, conceptual TV can be a source of ideas Limit to 1 hour
7–8 years	Lots of questions, and understanding ever greater	Two-wheel bike Interesting trips out Skate board, sport	Construction, puzzles, computer games Music lessons	Need for peer play Sports clubs Board games	Costumes of TV and video characters Special collections	Variety of drawing and art materials	Regular change of books from library or school

Helping a child learn the art of happiness

Children learn happiness and unhappiness from their own experiences and from the beliefs and attitudes of the people who take care of them. They learn to be loved and to be loving, and these tendencies can affect them in life-long ways. We live in a culture that places a great deal of emphasis on individual rights and personal responsibility but beliefs around happiness are not very clear. On one hand we are told happiness is possible, on the other we are bombarded with information that serves to feed and cultivate our unhappiness.

Interestingly, however, there is a lot of evidence that happy optimistic people are as effective, if not more effective, as unhappy pessimistic people in responding constructively to challenges. So parents and carers have a choice about the messages they give to their children.

Although you are not the only influence on your child, you are a very important part of those influences. It may be tricky, but in order to help your child learn the art of happiness, you may need to first start with yourself!

Some important things to remember

▲ You can't easily help a child experience happiness if you don't prioritise happiness yourself. Try deciding to become happier.

▲ Privilege, wealth and expensive extras are not necessary for happiness, nor is success in school or in exams. Many very successful people and very rich people are not happy.

▲ Some beliefs make happiness very difficult, others make it easier.

▲ Children and adults can need encouragement and permission to feel happy now. Many people think that they must do something else first in order to deserve or achieve happiness.

▲ Beliefs can change.

▲ Happiness needs self-esteem, and self-esteem needs a good relationship with the self. This usually develops from good relationships with others.

▲ Many people describe experiencing happiness when they are 'in flow' with an activity. In childhood, children commonly experience flow and discover the connection with themself during self-directed play. Play is very important!

▲ Mastery of something that you enjoy is another important route to happiness. Mastery can be experienced in the course of many activities, eg, sport, cooking, playing an instrument, drawing or painting, pursuing any hobby.

▲ Even people with extreme experiences of trauma, abandonment or neglect in childhood can still find happiness and fulfilment when they change their beliefs about themselves.

▲ For further ideas on happiness the books *Smart Love* by Martha and William Pieper, and *Happiness is a Choice* by Barry Neil Kaufman, are both highly recommended.

Happiness and choice – the role of beliefs

It is commonly believed that things that happen to us *cause* us to feel certain things, and act in certain ways.

STIMULUS		RESPONSE
She called me names	$\longrightarrow$	*I felt sad and I hit her*
He left me out of the game	$\longrightarrow$	*I felt hurt and upset*

We now know this idea is incorrect. Happiness and sadness or joy and anger are not inevitable products of the things that happen to us. Our feelings and behaviours arise as a consequence of our *beliefs* that are triggered by the stimulus.

STIMULUS	BELIEF	RESPONSE
She called me names	*I knew she didn't mean it*	*I ignored her*
He left me out of the game	*He thought I had hurt my leg*	*I felt OK*

What this means is that beliefs affect our feelings and behaviour in deep and profound ways.

How do beliefs develop?

➤ Beliefs develop from the earliest days of life, and even at a pre-verbal stage, as the young child tries to make sense of the world and *keep safe*. The child seeks patterns and draws conclusions about the world and themselves.

➤ Beliefs also develop as a result of the things that key carers tell the child about the world and about themselves.

➤ Beliefs are acquired from the dominant culture in which the child lives.

Beliefs that have a good or bad label attached to them are particularly powerful and are known as judgements. Judging something as bad is commonly linked to feelings of unhappiness.

The adoption of any belief involves a choice, ie, what to believe and what not to believe. What this means is that if you want to change a belief at any time, you can!

Beliefs that support happiness

Happiness starts with beliefs that support a positive relationship of the person with him or herself. This is known as self-esteem. Here are some beliefs that support happiness in children and adults.

I know people who love me and like being with me.
I can choose my beliefs about myself and about the world.
I am choosing to do what is important to me.
When I am lost there are people I can turn to.

Why play is so important to happiness

Play in childhood is critical to happiness. Children only play freely and enjoy their own company when they given enough opportunities to do so, and when they feel really relaxed in themselves and in their relationships. It is when children are relaxed that they can begin to discover their own wants, interests and pleasures, and their connection with their own self.

Why mastery is so important

Mastery is the experience that occurs when a person has worked at or practised something that matters to them and finally cracked it! A child who experiences plenty of mastery, particularly if it arises out of self-directed play and practice, will experience an increase in self-esteem with or without praise from others. Encourage interests that help the child to really explore who they are, not those in which they are simply acting to please others. Mastery supports optimism, and optimism is another link to happiness.

Changing unhelpful beliefs

Changing unhelpful beliefs, particularly those that are long-held, can be – but not always – straightforward. *Beliefs have a purpose in helping the person.* Generally speaking, beliefs learned early in life are more resistant to change than those learned later in life. As a parent you can model for your child the principal that:

➤ Beliefs can change.

➤ Some beliefs support happiness and confidence more than others.

➤ It is a good idea to get help to work on unhelpful beliefs.

17 Supporting your child's self-confidence, self-esteem and optimism

Children and adults have strengths and weaknesses. They vary in their abilities to do different things. However, it is now well-known that to be happy and successful, self-esteem, self-confidence and optimism are *very* important.

Although parents cannot control what happens to children, they do have a critically important role to play in how children feel and think about themselves. The feelings and thoughts that the child develops about him or herself in the first relationships with parents often strongly influence their approach to relationships with friends and other adults. An optimistic style of thinking gives a child the ability to bounce back after setbacks.

This leaflet will explain how you can help yourself or your child.

Some points to remember

▲ Young children are totally dependent on their parents and carers. They have an inbuilt need to seek their parent's positive attention and affection, to impress them and to please them. If these needs for attention, affection, approval and admiration are reliably met from key adults, the child will develop strong self-esteem and self-confidence.

▲ If a child's needs for attention, affection, approval and admiration are not reliably met, or if the parent or teacher often seems disinterested, unhappy or not impressed with the child, the child can begin to believe that the parent or teacher no longer likes or wants to care for them. Their self-esteem and self-confidence can become damaged and the child may become anxious, depressed, angry or resentful.

▲ Your child will take his or her first experiences of relationships with key adults into their relationships with friends and other adults.

▲ Children with poor self-esteem and self-confidence often have parents with poor self-esteem and self-confidence. One way to help your child is to think about what you can do to help yourself. Trying out some new thinking may be the first important step.

▲ An optimistic thinking style can be learned and will protect your child from depression, by giving them the ability to bounce back after the inevitable knocks and setbacks of life.

▲ Friendly cuddles, a hug, a back rub or tickle tell your children more effectively than words about your feelings for them.

▲ Encourage and support all of your child's efforts to do things with more independence.

▲ Work on building your *own* self-confidence and skills!

What are optimistic ways of thinking?

An optimistic style of thinking about events will give your child an ability to bounce back after the set-backs and inevitable knocks of life. Optimism may not always appear 'realistic' but it will protect your child from anxiety and depression. For example:

Bad events for pessimistic thinkers are commonly:
Permanent, affect everything and/or caused by others

Good events for pessimistic thinkers are commonly:
Temporary, very limited, and/or caused by others.

Bad events for optimistic thinkers are usually:
Temporary, limited in impact and/or caused by others.

Good events for optimistic thinkers are commonly:
Permanent, generally available, and/or caused by themself.

It is never too late to develop more optimism. Here are some ways you can help your child:

▲ Frequently telling your child you love them
▲ Showing your affection by friendly cuddles or hugs
▲ Spending time with them on things they enjoy
▲ Letting your child help you with things
▲ Taking the time to listen carefully and respectfully
▲ Discouraging your child's self put-downs
▲ Helping your child talk through and solve problems
▲ Helping your child to think positively
▲ Modelling positive self-talk
▲ Standing up for them when they need support
▲ Helping your child find his or her talents
▲ Supporting your child as they build and maintain relationships
▲ Helping your child learn the skills of daily living
▲ Encouraging your child to persevere after set-backs

What are self-esteem and self-confidence?

Self-esteem, self-confidence and optimism are closely related to one another, but are subtly different.

High self-esteem is related to liking and trusting yourself as you are. The first and most important people that we get our sense of self-esteem from are our parents. It is often related to optimism.

Low self-esteem is related to not liking and trusting yourself as you are. Self-esteem can be damaged when:

▲ parents or others are often critical or neglecting of a child
▲ a child feels compared unfavourably with others
▲ parents make no time to be with the child, or let them down
▲ parents undermine things that are important to the child

High self-confidence comes from knowing that you can achieve the things that you want to achieve. It grows out of the *experience* of trying new things and being successful. Part of self-confidence is knowing that even if there are set-backs and difficulties that it is worth persevering.

Low self-confidence comes from believing that you can't achieve what you want to achieve, and the belief that you can't be a winner. Low self-confidence develops from the experience of too much failure or too little success. Low self-confidence is often related to pessimism.

Confidence can be damaged when:

▲ The child's environment is not adapted to his or her developmental needs
▲ There is not enough support and praise for the child
▲ Parents or others appear to only value perfect results
▲ Parents believe the child will be unable to cope, and say so
▲ There are big changes or events in the child's world that the child doesn't understand and feels powerless to control

18 Building your child's self-esteem and confidence

Graded responsibilities

As a parent your main task is to prepare your child to be a happy and effective adult. So the most important thing you must do is to make sure that you pay attention to your child's inner and outer sense of self-esteem and self-confidence.

Your child's inner self-esteem can only come from knowing that you care for him or her reliably and unconditionally as a unique and special person. But your child's outer self-confidence comes from knowing that he or she has grown-up skills and competence, and can therefore play a useful and appreciated role in the day-to-day life of the family and community. So your child needs practice with the range of tasks that adults need to carry out. It is so much easier to take on responsibilities gradually and steadily than all at once when you turn sixteen. This leaflet will give you some ideas about the ways in which you can build your child's skills.

Some points to remember

▲ Young children love to help adults and to join in with them. If you want your child to become a responsible adult, the easiest time to start is therefore as young as possible.

▲ Introduce jobs and responsibilities gradually, and in the beginning always help your child and always keep the activities short. If you make the tasks too long or difficult, you will put your child off helping.

▲ Criticism of your child will not develop his or her self-esteem and self-confidence. Try whenever you possibly can to be as supportive, and encouraging as possible. You may sometimes have to be very firm and do things with them if they are still very reluctant. A reluctant child may need more time from you.

▲ Make sure that your child knows exactly what is expected of him in the job so that he or she can gain the satisfaction of a job well done.

▲ Some families like to link pocket money to the idea of jobs that have to be done. Money can for example be earned by fulfilling responsibilities appropriate to the child's developmental age. *Required jobs* are thus the ones that are appropriate to your child's developmental age and that you expect them to do regularly. *Bonus jobs* may even be able to earn extra pocket money!

▲ Make sure that you always appreciate your child's helpful actions in the home. This will be the best sort of reliable reward for them.

▲ Always remember to adapt your demands to your child's individual needs and the specific circumstances you are in.

▲ Be patient and flexible and remember though it may seem like hard work at first to get your children participating in jobs at home, in the long-run *everyone* will benefit!

Building self-esteem and confidence through responsibilities   Here are some ideas about appropriate responsibilities for your child's age

Developmental age	Personal hygiene and clothes	Own room	House and garden	Mealtimes	Caring for and helping others	Out and about	Homework	Money
3–4 years (with lots of help)	Brush own teeth Wash hands and face Wash after toilet Help put clean clothes away	Notice need to tidy Help tidy own room and put away toys Know where things go	Notice jobs that need doing Help out on small tasks and errands	Wash hands Help lay table Help simple preparation Pass plates round	Assist others who need it – 5 min tasks Make cards for others Help feed pets	Walk holding hands Know to stop at road junctions Say hello to people when we meet	Play alone/with friends and talk about the world as much as possible Look at books with adults every day	Choose how to spend a small amount Know some items have to be saved up for
5–6 years (with support)	Match socks and put dirty clothes in laundry Fold clothes and put in agreed place Face/hands clean Help clean shoes	Start to tidy certain items without help Straighten bed clothes Put cassette tapes in correct boxes	Help tidy bathroom (towels/toothbrushes, etc) Bring in outside toys and games Take rubbish bags out	Lay table accurately with given items Put dirty pots to wash Wash and dry a few unbreakable dishes Help with dishwasher Prepare cold snacks	Assist others – 10 min tasks Feed pets without help Help clean out pets Know how to say sorry	Remain close to adults when out Understand Stop, Look and Listen Aware of stranger risk Answer phone well	Play and talk lots Sing and make music Read aloud to adult every day Practise 5 spellings Practise 5 sums	Find things on adults shopping list Find things the same that cost different prices Start to earn small amount of money
7–9 years (more independence)	Bath/shower and wash own hair Usually check and choose own clothes to wear Clean own shoes	Straighten books or boxes Keep own room tidy Take sheets off bed Vacuum own room Carefully put away own clothes	Turn lights off Carefully sweep an area inside/outside Clean and tidy bathroom after use Clean bathroom sink Plant items in garden	Set accurately table, finding most items Peel or chop vegetables Help prepare recipes Load and unload dishwasher or wash up	Assist others – 20 min tasks Send cards or letters Feed or clean out pets Sort out conflicts with friends or siblings	Be able to cross some roads alone Recognise dangers First independent trips to friends/local shops/school Phone friends	Find out about the world Play and talk lots Sing and make music Read aloud 3x week Practise spellings Practise tables/sums	Start to be able to supplement pocket money with money for other small jobs Open an account
10–12 years (desired items can be earned)	Help with purchase of own clothes Save up extra money for desired 'designer labels' Have regular exercise Iron a few items	Sometimes (change own sheets) Dust shelves Clean bedroom windows Clean and tidy own cupboards	Sometimes sort washing Help hang/fold washing Help mow lawn Wash the car Weed small area	Make hot drinks, hot snacks Bake a cake or dessert Make a simple meal Be aware of healthy balanced diet and exercise	Assist others who need it – 30 min task Take dog for walk Know how to be proactive in friendships – treating others respectfully but standing ground	Run errands to local shops for items Know about drugs, alcohol, peer pressure and keeping safe Know when to ask for adult help	Write down tasks Start promptly Work carefully Ask for help if needed Finish on time Check work Hand it in	Keep records of income or expenditure Look for small income earning tasks with friends Sell on used items Start to save up for larger items
13–15 years	Shop for own clothes Try make-up Check own body odour	Help redecorate own room Design look of own room	Mop floors Clean windows Mow lawn Help with car repairs	Buy items for a meal Prepare a balanced meal Try out new recipes	Assist others who need it – longer jobs Babysit for short periods	Come home at agreed times Know about sexuality and keeping safe	Complete work expected by school Prepare properly for exams	Pocket money tied to responsibilities Work to a budget Paper round
16 plus	Take care of all clothing and hygiene decisions	Take care of own affairs	Take fair adult share of cooking, cleaning, tidying, etc	Regularly prepare a meal Clear up after a meal	Take part in helping others in the community	Take responsibility for own safety with adult in background	Complete tasks expected by college/work	Do outside jobs for money Contribute to house expenses

19

Helping your child develop concentration skills and maturity

It is common for parents to feel that their children have poor skills in attention and concentration. But did you know that concentration is something that develops slowly? Children develop these skills at different rates. Boys commonly take longer to develop concentration on tasks involving fine motor skills.

Concentration skills are important as they linked to maturity and to success in school and work. Some persistent concentration difficulties are thought to be linked to subtle perceptual or co-ordination difficulties. Sometimes poor concentration can be linked to a history of anxiety, and/or a hypersensitivity to failure. As a parent you can help your child develop these skills, but it is necessary to make time to help your child build their skills via very small steps and a great deal of supported, preferably daily practice.

This leaflet is intended to give you some ideas to of the sorts of activities that will help your child improve his or her concentration.

Some points to remember

▲ There are very few children who cannot concentrate at all. There are many children who concentrate on some things and not on others, or in some settings and not in others.

▲ Try to be specific:

– Start by making a list of the situations/activities in which you observe your child giving very *good* concentration. Compliment your child for these skills!

– Now, what sort of tasks does your child have difficulty concentrating on? Are these difficulties causing your child problems now, or will they later?

▲ Use the ideas inside this leaflet to select one or two skills that could help. Discuss your reasons with your child. They might like to choose their own skills.

▲ Make some time to help your child learn the new skill. Stick to the following rules for success:

– Choose a distraction free time and place, turn the television off.

– Stay involved, without doing the task for your child

– The tasks should initially be age appropriate and/or easy so that you are sure that your child can experience success. The sessions should be short but regular and you may initially need to be very firm (straight after school before fun is a good time)

– *Always* praise your child's successes in learning new skills requiring concentration and perseverance.

▲ At first your child will probably need a lot of help and supervision from you. Gradually they will need less help. Eventually your child will carry out the skills independently. Always insist that jobs are finished, before moving on.

▲ Plenty of physical activity and a regular healthy diet are vital for children with concentration difficulties. Some of the best concentration can arise just a meal or after a good play outside.

▲ Some children benefit from some very structured exercise programmes. Others benefit from medication or dietary changes. If you are unsure, seek professional advice.

▲ With patience and perseverance from you, your child's concentration skills and maturity will flower!

Developing concentration skills

Children with concentration problems often have weak skills in the following areas. They are all things that can be learned with practice. Use the lists to identify skills that might help your child. Remember to be very positive about how much progress they are making. You might say...

'Look how well you concentrated on that ...'

'I can't believe how much progress you have made ...'

'Let's go and show ...'

Sport-based/movement activities

▲ climbing over a frame,

▲ hitting or kicking a ball with a bat/against a target

▲ taking turns in a ball game

▲ balancing on a narrow beam, or skateboard

▲ skipping with a rope for multiple jumps

School related skills

▲ board games or card games of any sort

▲ accurately colouring in a picture

▲ drawing/copying a simple picture looking carefully at details

▲ completing a simple jigsaw in a short time

▲ using a ruler with precision

▲ forming letters correctly or writing with neat handwriting

▲ completing a page of very simple sums in a short time

▲ tidying own toys away at the end of an activity

▲ listening to a story read aloud and talking about it

▲ building a model in Lego/ Meccano

▲ making something/cutting out accurately with scissors

▲ making a list or a plan for the day

Home responsibilities

▲ getting undressed quickly and sorting clothes

▲ getting dressed quickly and accurately

▲ folding clothes or hanging up washing

▲ putting away shopping

▲ laying the table

▲ washing up/drying up

▲ loading or unloading the dishwasher

▲ vacuuming or sweeping a room carefully

▲ tidying a room or making a bed

▲ caring for a pet

▲ inventing own play ideas (not waiting for others)

Social skills

▲ stopping and listening when others are talking

▲ looking at the person who is talking

▲ speaking clearly so others can understand

▲ waiting and not interrupting when others are talking

▲ sitting at the table through a meal

▲ walking next to someone without running off

▲ going into a shop and not picking items off shelves

▲ having a two-way listening conversation

▲ taking an accurate message

▲ answering the phone clearly/making a phone call

Conflict resolution skills

▲ thinking through the consequences of actions

▲ listening accurately to what someone else is saying

▲ expressing own views and needs with words

▲ thinking of different solutions to problems

20 Helping babies and young children to develop good sleep patterns

Some babies fall easily into a sleep pattern that is comfortable for their parents. Some children need more active help to develop good sleep patterns.

Illness, holidays, teething or stress in the family can often disturb a child's sleep patterns and children commonly need support in beginning to sleep more regularly again.

However most babies who have sleep or settling difficulties can be helped if their parents persevere using a few key ideas. This leaflet offers some ways you can help your child.

Some points to remember

⚔ To help babies sleep well there are five things to remember.
   - Try to stick to some regular sleep times if possible.
   - Develop a settling routine
   - Help your child learn to fall asleep without you present
   - Interact with your child during the day not the night.
   - Persevere.

⚔ The amount of sleep that babies needs varies and changes over time:
   - 0–6 months: one or two wakings in the night, two or three naps each day
   - 6–15 months: one waking in the night, one or two naps in the day
   - 15–24 months: Sleeping through some nights, one daytime nap
   - 2–4 years: 11–12 hours at night and one daytime nap.
   - 5–6 years: 11–12 hours at night.

⚔ Most children find it difficult to sleep when they have become over-tired. If your child isn't sleeping at least ensure there is a rest time.

⚔ Some young babies do cry a lot when they are small. Tell yourself simply that he or she is simply a child who doesn't sleep well *at the moment*. Keep using the same principles because at a certain point your perseverance will pay off.

⚔ If your child's sleep problems are very persistent, you are probably feeling very tired and irritable. If at all possible find a way to take turns with someone else. Let someone else do some of the getting up some of the time.

⚔ Persistent sleep problems sometimes go along with post-natal anxiety and depression. The baby picks up the adult's unhappiness or worrying and finds it harder to feel relaxed enough to go to sleep. But the parent feels more and more exhausted and this contributes to the anxiety and the depression. If you think you might be experiencing post-natal depression it is important to get help as soon as possible.

If your baby cries a lot

▲ Make sure your baby is gaining weight steadily. A hungry baby will cry more. If you are breast feeding, take care to rest and eat carefully. Regular expressing of milk from early on can help your milk supply stay high.

▲ Make sure your baby has a calm routine with enough sleep and is not becoming overtired or over stimulated. An overtired child will find it difficult to sleep

▲ Encourage your baby to develop a link to a soother for sleep-time. This might be a special blanket, or teddy. Some children like a dummy.

▲ When your baby wakes, *listen carefully to the cry.* It is best not to respond to little grumbles – they may go back to sleep. If the grumbles are more intense, keep the light off and go to reassure your baby – help him or her to find their soother, feed if absolutely necessary or check if there is a painful wind bubble. But do so in the dark with as little fuss as possible, before settling back to sleep. Play is for daylight hours.

▲ Many unsettled babies find movement very soothing. A few moments of gentle patting, or rocking or a pushchair or car ride, can help your baby to make the transition to a relaxed state from which they can fall asleep.

▲ Colic or persistent crying in the early months and at the end of the day often arises from the immaturity of the baby's nervous system. If you have tried everything and nothing works, don't be afraid to let your baby have a good 15–20 minute cry in their own room. The effect for your baby is like having an exhausting run, helping them discharge tension and relax more fully the next time you try to help them settle.

▲ Early morning wakers benefit from the same approach. Invest in blackout curtains, and if you have to go to your baby, say and do as little as possible, feed only if necessary and return him or her to their own bed until your preferred waking time. If your baby is not awake at 7.00 am it is best to wake them up and start your usual routine.

Understanding very young babies' sleep patterns

Sleeping and waking is organised in cycles. Babies have periods of deep sleep and light sleep. To help your baby develop good sleep patterns, you must work with these natural cycles and work towards making sure that he or she is able to fall asleep *without* you being present.

Observe closely. Does your baby have a natural rhythm that suits you both? If not here is a simple routine that suits many babies from four months to two or three years of age

7.00 am	Get baby up to start the day, have a first feed
8.00 am	Breakfast
8.45–9.30 am	Put baby for sleep in quiet room or pushchair[1]
10.00 am	ACTIVITY TIME – Wake baby if necessary
11.30 am	Lunch
12.15 pm	Afternoon sleep – quiet dark room if possible[2]
2.30 pm	ACTIVITY TIME
4.00 pm	snack
4.30–5.00 pm	Short late afternoon sleep, wake if necessary[3]
5.30 pm	Supper
6.00 pm	Play in a warm bath and books or songs
7.00pm	Settled to sleep in own room

As children get older the early morning and late afternoon sleeps are usually dropped. Routines also commonly change with holidays and illness and outings. However, you can always return to a routine if the basic pattern exists.

Notes

1 This sleep may not be needed after 9–12 months
2 Many babies need this sleep until 2–2½ years of age
3 This sleep often dips around 3–4 months

Helping children eat well

Helping a child learn to eat well and to enjoy healthy food, is one of the earliest challenges of parenting. Parents often worry that their child isn't eating enough, or enough of the right things. As they are worried, they may begin to go to great lengths to ensure their child eats *something* – anything! Unfortunately, these efforts often backfire: mealtimes may become times of great stress and tension for adults and children.

However, mealtimes *can* be a pleasant time of sharing between children and adults. Children can gradually become interested in food and in what they eat, and they can, over time, become less fussy eaters. Mealtimes don't need to be a problem forever.

This leaflet will give you some ideas about how you might help your child to develop good eating habits.

Some points to remember

▲ If there is a calm, unstressed atmosphere around food, children will always eat as much as they need to – remember this can sometimes be very little.

▲ It is not a good idea to offer young children too many choices in what they eat. Too much choice encourages fussiness rather than good eating habits.

▲ Children's appetites vary. Some children eat a lot, some children eat less. Children sometimes eat very little for a few weeks and then a lot at other times.

▲ Mild illnesses such as coughs and colds and flu can affect a child's appetite. Don't worry, just reduce the portions until the appetite returns.

▲ Encourage the habit of finishing what is on the plate. This means always starting with small portions that a child can happily finish.

▲ Children need regular drinks, at every meal-time and at snack times. Stick to water or fruit juices and avoid very sugary drinks.

▲ Constipation can affect a child's appetite. It is important to check that your child has a diet that has enough roughage and liquid so that stools pass regularly – at least once every two days.

▲ It is not a good idea to let a reluctant eater fill up with sweets and desserts. Establish a pattern of only having sweets or desserts if the main savoury dish has been finished first.

▲ If your child has a weight problem, it is much better to establish a routine for the whole family of starting to eat healthier tasty foods than to put your child on a formal diet.

▲ Keep calm but persevere. If you have not made too much of it, as children get older they often become less fussy or picky over time.

Some tips for establishing good eating habits

▲ Have a regular routine for meals. If the meals are regular, the child will feel the sensations of hunger and be more willing to eat.

Eg:
8.00	Breakfast
10.30	Mid-morning snack
12.00	Lunch
3.30	Mid-afternoon snack
5.30	Tea/supper
7.00	Bed-time snack

▲ Encourage your child to sit at a table to eat, and turn the television off. This will help your child to concentrate on eating.

▲ Try to eat with your child at least some of the time, and make meal-times a pleasant family time for talking.

▲ Try not to let your child graze between meals and snacks. This will cut their appetite for meals.

▲ Give a reluctant eater *small* portions only (even sometimes just a teaspoon of each different thing) that they can *finish*. Having too much on the plate can put a child off eating. Your child will prefer to eat a little and be able to ask for more.

▲ Remember that the majority of young children will *express* an automatic dislike for any food that is different or unfamiliar, even without trying it. Don't over-react! This doesn't mean your child is a fussy eater. In general, remember that children like familiar foods with familiar tastes and textures.

▲ Encourage your child to try small amounts of a variety of foods from an early age, as this will help them become used to new flavours.

▲ Always praise your child for finishing and trying new things.

The child who refuses to eat or is very fussy

Parents can get very anxious or tense when a child shows no interest in food or refuses it. However, becoming tense and pressurising a child, or giving too many choices, can make the difficulties worse. Here are some additional tips:

▲ Re-establish a clear routine for meals and snacks and serve only *very* small amounts of healthy food that you know your child likes – always include some simple basics such as pasta, potatoes or bread.

▲ If your child finishes the food on the plate, look very impressed and praise your child. You might say: 'Wow! What a Good Eater you are today!'

▲ If your child says they don't want the food or just plays with the food:
 - *Don't* nag, shout or get angry.
 - *Don't* try to force feed.
 - *Don't* offer another choice
 - And remember, *stay calm.*

▲ Leave the plate of food with the child for 10 minutes. Calmly ask once more if they want it. If they say 'No', remind them there will be *no dessert and nothing* until the next mealtime. *Then just take the food away.*

▲ If your child changes their mind a few minutes later, *avoid* giving in and bringing the food back. Remind them they will be able to eat something at the next meal.

▲ *Very* gradually introduce new foods into your child's diet. Remember to frequently tell them how very impressed you are with their new eating habits.

Note: You will need to persevere with this strategy for weeks rather than days, but with a long view the difficulties *will* be resolved.

22 Playing with your baby: helping your baby and yourself

Caring for a baby is always very demanding on parent's time. But some babies are more demanding to parent than other babies. Some babies' development seems rather slow; some seem rather disinterested in other people; others never seem to be content. In these situations the parents can feel that the child gives very little back. It is not uncommon for parents to sometimes feel worn out, exasperated and resentful towards their child. Something is needed to make things more positive.

This leaflet explains how regular short periods of baby-centred play-time can help your baby's development *and* help develop a more positive relationship between you.

Some points to remember

⧩ Some babies are more challenging to parent than other babies. Some babies are very active, or unsettled, others react in very intense ways to things. Attention, language and play skills also develop more slowly in some babies than in others. By carefully watching, helping and joining in with your baby, you will build your relationship and help your baby to develop.

⧩ It is common for parents to be completely worn out and exasperated with their babies at times. If there are also other stresses on you or the family this makes parenting harder. Being worn out is often expressed as anger, irritability and impatience towards the baby. But if irritability and impatience starts to happen a lot in a relationship, with a baby it will tend to make the baby's behaviour worse.

⧩ If you are often irritable or impatient it can be a useful sign that you need to prioritise getting yourself more support or more breaks, as well as a sign that you need to find ways to try to make your relationship with this baby more positive.

⧩ Watching too much television will seriously delay the development of your child's language, attention and play skills. Try to stick to half an hour a day of programmes designed for young children until your child is 4–5 years old. Sometimes you will need to use television as a 'baby-sitter' but remember, it helps *you*, not your baby.

⧩ It is not helpful to give your baby your full attention *all* the time. They can develop an 'addiction' to it and subsequently find it more difficult to play independently. Independent play is another vital skill.

Why do babies need baby-led time?

Babies *need* attention from parents and others. They need to know that their parents are interested in them and will help out when needed. By giving full positive attention to their babies, even for short periods, parents show their babies that they care for and respect them. It shows them that the world of people is interesting and enjoyable. This is usually enough to help the baby feel more relaxed the rest of the time. But the parent can also help develop many of the baby's skills during this baby-led time.

When babies do not have short periods of full positive attention from parents, their development can be affected. They do not have the benefit of the parent's knowledge about the world, but they can often also feel more anxious and uncertain about whether the parent really cares for them.

Babies who are not sure about whether their parents have positive feelings for them can become 'attention-seeking'. They can find ways to gain attention through demanding behaviour that they have discovered will at least get a reaction from adults. Or they may appear to not care about the parent, expressing disinterest or resistance to the parent's attempts to interact.

Baby play-time can therefore help you and your baby:

▲ If you currently have a difficult or strained relationship with your baby

▲ If your baby has delays in language, attention or play skills

In a short baby led play session, we aim to give our full positive attention to the baby, adapting our own behaviour to fit in with what the baby is interested in. *During this time, we are not asking the baby to fit in with our interests.* Remember that fitting in with adults is very difficult for most young babies.

Baby play sessions: watch, wait and wonder.

The setting

▲ Find a *quiet* place to be with your baby on a one-to-one.

▲ Try to make sure that you will not be distracted

▲ You can often be your baby's most interesting play companion, but also have a range of simple toys available including noise makers and picture books.

▲ Position yourself with your baby so as to make eye contact possible.

The activities

▲ *Watch* your baby carefully. What is he/she interested in or trying to do? Can you help or join in?

▲ Find ways to join in, help and gently extend your child's understanding of the world by making their focus of attention even more interesting. For example:

– *help him or her to learn that other people can be fun:* sing and make up turn taking games such as peek a boo. Don't be afraid to be silly, your baby will love it!

– *encourage watching and listening skills:* repeat clearly the sounds and words your baby uses, speaking slowly and clearly, adding new words for things that your baby is looking at and by using language that is just a bit more advanced than your baby's; Try not to ask questions.

– *extend their play skills* by showing enthusiasm and interest in your child's focus of attention, by adding new ideas into your child's chosen activity and by changing focus when your baby loses interest.

– *build your relationship* by smiling a lot, giving hugs, encouraging and praising your child and letting them know you are enjoying this time with them

Remember, any moment of the day is good baby time!

23 Helping young children learn to talk

People communicate with each other in two important ways. The first way is **non-verbal**, that is, without words, but with eye contact, face expressions, sounds and gestures. We learn to do this in the very first months of life, with support from our parents and first carers.

The second way that we communicate is verbally, that is, with words. Verbal skills usually develop in the second and third year of life. Children develop these skills at different rates and there are *some* children who find these skills very difficult. But most children learn language quite easily if they are given enough of the right opportunities. If your child is showing some delays, there are things that you can do to make a difference.

This leaflet explains about the development of communication skills and offers some ideas of how you can help your child.

Some points to remember

➤ Young children *cannot* develop good skills in language from the television or video. This is because the television does not listen carefully to them as an adult can. Too much television at an early age, without enough conversation, will affect your child's language development.

➤ Young children learn to communicate best by spending time with adults who are not too rushed, and who can talk clearly and listen carefully to them in a quiet environment.

➤ Good skills in language both in non-verbal and in verbal language skills make a big difference to children's experience in school. It is very difficult to learn to read, or to get on with others, if you are not yet confident at speaking.

➤ Young children who have delays in language skills often become much more frustrated, because they cannot express themselves easily. They are more likely to have temper tantrums or outbursts and may find it harder to work out solutions in playground games without fighting.

➤ Children begin learning to communicate from the moment they are first born. It is important to begin talking to them and singing to them from the very earliest days. The earlier you start the better.

➤ Some children develop language skills more easily than others, for example girls commonly learn to speak earlier than boys. But all children need as much chance as possible to hear clear language.

➤ Some children have very specific difficulties learning language. They have a language disability. The same basic methods will help these children, but, if you have any concern at all, ask for advice as early as possible from a speech therapist.

How language and communication skills develop

New born babies can communicate their needs through their crying. But when they are well-cared for, they usually quickly learn to communicate in a range of other ways as well. These skills develop gradually.

▲ Non-verbal communication skills (including 'emotional literacy/ understanding')

▲ Verbal communication skills

We now know that both are important, but that children may have difficulties in one or both areas. These skills develop gradually.

Stages in Non-Verbal Communication Skills:

1 day old	Baby cries to express discomfort and need for help
6 weeks	Baby has different cries for different needs e.g. hunger, boredom, being over-stimulated etc
16 weeks:	Makes eye contact and laughs with another person
9 months	Tugs on clothes to be picked up
	Follows a point or a person's direction of gaze
18 months	Can copy simple actions e.g. clapping, tongue out
	Can point or show something interesting to an adult

Stages in Verbal Communication Skills:

8 weeks	Responds to sound of a familiar voice, likes song
14 weeks	First sounds, blowing bubbles
9 months	Lots of babble with different repetitive sounds
	Loves 'sound conversations' with others
12 months	First familiar sounding words; ma-ma, da-da
16 months	Lots of single names for objects if supported by adults
22 months	Beginning to put two words together
30 months	Longer sentences, lots of talk, if supported
4 years	Talks a lot and can express quite complicated ideas, feelings and experiences using words

Helping your young child develop language

▲ Reduce confusing background noise and activity
- Make sure your child is often in a quiet calm place
- Turn the television off!
- Provide interesting sound makers to experiment with
- Ensure your child has one-to-one time with adults who talk clearly

▲ Show your child the social world can be fun
- Find short repetitive action games/songs your child loves
- Aim for 1 min shared focus, then build this up gradually
- Change activity when your child loses interest
- Encourage good eye contact and lots of laughing!

▲ Show your child how copying works
- Listen or watch and copy your child's sounds and actions (This strategy is called 'joining'- your child will love it!)
- DON'T pressure your child to copy you – this will come.

▲ Look out for your child's communications
- Give your child time to communicate with you
- Start to notice how your child expresses likes and dislikes

▲ Increase your use of simplified language:
- Speak more slowly and more clearly, use short sentences
- Notice what your child is looking at and name or describe it
- Look at favourite books together with simple pictures
- Add *detail* to what your child has noticed and can already say

▲ Use words to describe feelings
- Give your child words for feelings, his/hers and yours
- Talk about the feelings of characters in books

▲ Let your child lead: Don't rush or pressurise them
- Don't make an issue of correcting your child's speech
- Your child will stop talking if they feel under pressure
- Listen lots, and enjoy your child's progress!

24 Encouraging good behaviour

Some children seem to have no difficulty knowing how to behave in socially acceptable ways. Other children find it much harder. It is not helpful to think of them as naughty children because they can come to think of *themselves* as naughty. These children need more help 'to learn how to be good'.

As parents, we can help our children learn to behave in ways that will make them welcome in social places, with their friends and with other adults.

This leaflet offers you some ideas about how to help your child.

Some points to remember

▲ You can't change a child's behaviour with criticism and nagging.

▲ Young children are totally dependent on their parents. They have an in-built need to seek their parent's positive attention and affection, to impress them and to please them. Knowing that the parent or adult cares for them and listens to them, is a way in which they come to feel safe and confident in themselves.

▲ Young children also have a need to test things out and try to control things. So they need to know that their parents are reliable, in charge and are able to insist on things being done in a certain way. This is another way that they come to feel safe.

▲ If these two safety needs are met, your child will develop strong self-esteem and self-confidence. You have a very big role to play in building your child's self-esteem and self-image, and self-confidence

▲ If your relationship with any of your children is challenging, you must start by *making time to build a positive relationship with him or her.* Your child needs to know that you love and care for him or her as a unique person. You will only be able to have an influence on your child's behaviour if your child is sure about this. Don't compare your child with others.

▲ As a parent your most powerful tool is your attention:
 – A behaviour + attention = more of that behaviour
 – A behaviour + no attention = less of that behaviour

▲ It helps to try to be patient; young children need us to make time. If you know you can be more patient if you get a break from child care from time to time, make this a priority for yourself.

▲ Remember change happens gradually. Your child is maturing so with perseverance and consistency from you, things *will* improve!

Encouraging good behaviour

'I keep telling him but it never seems to make a difference'

Children *need* attention from others. Consequently, if they can not get it for behaving well, they may try to get it by behaving badly. Here are some tips to help you make sure your child gets your attention for the right things.

➤ **Catch your child being good.** Do you praise and notice every time your child keeps to your rules, and is behaving well?

➤ **Prevent 'bad behaviour' by careful planning.**

➤ **Make sure your child has enough varied activities to prevent naughtiness from boredom.** Young children need short periods of activity with plenty of variety.

➤ **Make sure your child knows your house rules and be consistent about enforcing them.** For example:
   – No hitting others
   – Ask before you use somebody else's things.

➤ **Face your child and speak to him or her in a firm calm voice when you have something important to say.**

➤ **Use the 'If ... Then' formula.** Children need to learn about the consequences of actions. The 'If you do X, then I will do Y' formula can be used for positive and for negative consequences

➤ **Follow through.** Your child needs to know that you mean what you say. If you ask your child to do something reasonable you *must* see it through and insist that he or she do as you have asked.

Discouraging bad behaviour

If you wish to discourage bad behaviour you must work out what behaviour you want instead.

➤ **Make sure your child knows what specific behaviours you don't like and what specific behaviours you want more of.** When you are going into a challenging situation (like shopping or a visit to a friend), try to talk with your child about what you do and don't want from them

➤ **Practice the skill of acting fierce and spelling out your rules whilst staying calm inside.** Children know the difference between a calm strict adult and an angry adult but respect the former.

➤ **Ignore or play down little naughtinesses.** Every child does some naughty things some of the time. Wherever possible it is best to ignore these or pay as little attention as possible. If you spend a lot of time talking about naughty behaviour it will increase. Try to concentrate on talking about your child's *positive* behaviours

➤ **Use distraction when you see your child building up to bad behaviour.** Young children with a short attention span need your help in finding appropriate interesting activities that keep them out of trouble.

➤ **Make sure your child knows that hitting and shouting is not a good way of solving problems.** Show your child how to sort out conflicts with words not fists. This can take years of practising!

➤ **Make sure your child knows that he or she will not get their own way by having a tantrum.** As far as possible try to ignore tantrums: Say as little as possible, turn away or move away, or insist your child goes in another room to cool off. Stay calm yourself. Insist on words and respect. Move as quickly as you can to a positive focus.

➤ **Don't laugh at your child's anti-social behaviour** as this will encourage it.

25 Encouraging good behaviour in children with disabilities

When parents discover that their child has a physical disability or a learning disability they are often shocked and upset. There are a lot of adjustments to make. Sometimes parents find that they feel confused about the right way to manage their child's behaviour. They are not sure whether their child should be treated in the same way as other children or in special ways.

This leaflet looks at the special issues that arise in managing the behaviour of children with disabilities. It offers some ideas of how you can help yourself and your child.

Some points to remember

▲ Every child is unique. A developmental assessment will help you understand more about your child's current level of skills. If a child's behaviour is very challenging, it is often useful to think about their needs in terms of a much younger child.

▲ It is particularly important to try to understand *how* your child communicates, and what he or she currently understands. A child with poor communication skills will communicate feelings with their behaviour. Always look at ways to increase your understanding of what your child is telling you and your child's ability to communicate effectively with you and others.

▲ Children with disabilities have some special needs that often require us to be more patient and understanding but in many ways their needs are just the same as other children. In many aspects of their lives, they do not need special handling.

▲ Children with disabilities need supportive, loving relationships with the adults that care for them. They need adults to demonstrate their confidence in them. With this support, they will be able to overcome many of their difficulties.

▲ Caring for a child with a disability is more demanding than caring for an average child. It is important to try to find ways to get regular breaks for yourself to recharge your own batteries. This may not always be easy but is necessary.

▲ Though their care is undoubtedly more demanding, many parents of older children with disabilities feel that having a child with a disability changed their life in positive ways that they couldn't have predicted.

▲ If you feel you need additional advice, don't hesitate to contact your GP, health visitor or child development service.

Understanding the behaviour of children with disabilities

Children with disabilities are special in that there are certain things that they find much more difficult to do than average children. If they have a physical disability it may be difficult for them to move around easily. If they have a learning disability their language or social skills may be developing more slowly than other children.

It is important for us to take these special needs into account. However, it is also important to remember that, in many ways, children with disabilities are just like other children. There are things that they need to learn. For example, like other children they need to learn that other people have needs too.

If you are a parent of a child with a disability you have a challenging job to do. You will need to take your child's special needs into account, but you also need to help your child to develop in ways that will increase his or her long-term independence, confidence and maturity. This includes gradually helping the child learn to behave in socially acceptable ways within the family.

Some parents find it very difficult to say 'No' to a child with a disability as they feel guilty or worry that their child can't understand. But it is very important to say 'No' sometimes, and to be firm, as you would with any other child, otherwise the child with a disability can become a little tyrant in the family. Parents and brothers and sisters become exhausted and resentful.

If your child's behaviour is quite challenging to manage it is important to carry out a 'developmental assessment'. This will help you work out a developmental age for your child. It will also help you work out which skills your child currently needs help with. Children with difficult behaviour often have weak skills in attention, language and independent play.

Encouraging good behaviour

To encourage mature and socially acceptable behaviour in children with disabilities we need to use exactly the same principles that we use with average children. These include the following:

▲ Take your child's developmental age into account (developmentally less mature children require considerably more patience as their attention, language, and play skills are less developed)

▲ Prioritise activities that will increase your child's attention, language and independent play skills. Half an hour a day of undivided attention from you on things that your child wants to do will do wonders! Supporting one-to-one play dates with other children can help a great deal.

▲ Always look for the positives. Use as much praise and encouragement as you can. Criticism doesn't change behaviour.

▲ Don't be afraid to be firm. Children with disabilities also need you to be able to say 'No' and set limits.

▲ Give your child plenty of warning about what is going to happen: talk it through or explain events in ways that he or she will understand. Using pictures can help.

▲ Find ways to build your child's skills in independent living and self-confidence with others whenever you can. Your child will need this confidence.

▲ As far as possible ignore small naughtinesses. Use distraction and move on quickly to a positive focus. Build up your child's alternative behaviour skills.

Some points to remember

▲ Many children need active help in learning how to behave in socially acceptable ways.

▲ Avoid using negative labels such as 'naughty', 'lazy', 'careless' or 'thoughtless' to describe your child. Your child will come to think of him or herself this way. This makes it difficult for your child and for you.

▲ 'Good behaviour' is made up of lots of small details. You must show your child what these details are and pay attention to them by describing them whenever your child does any of them. Remind your child of past incidents of success.

▲ It is hard work learning to behave well. If your child has had a good day, and then had a lapse or made a mistake, don't draw too much attention to the lapse, emphasise the positives.

▲ Wherever possible use positive labels to describe behaviours that you have seen. For example, labels such as perseverance, patience, kindness, generosity, carefulness, thoughtfulness all give a child a positive sense of their own self.

▲ Help your child learn to praise themself! Help them to identify what things they are really working on at present. A child who can say positive things about him or herself is more ready to enter into relationships in a positive way.

▲ Always encourage effort and progress not final results. Children need to feel that it is possible to overcome difficulties by perseverance and that you believe they can do something.

26 Using praise effectively

Many parents know that children like, and need, praise and encouragement. We commonly hear parents telling children that they have been 'good'. But parents don't always know what else to say. However, praise is a very powerful tool – it can involve much more than telling a child that he or she has been good. With a little practice, you can use targeted praise to bring about many positive changes in your family environment.

This leaflet looks at the area of praise in more depth and explains how you can use it to help yourself and your child

Why criticism doesn't work

When we become exasperated with our children we often criticise them and label their behaviour in negative ways. For example parents can often be heard to describe their children as follows:

- 'She's so slow'
- 'He's a really selfish person'
- 'He never takes care of his things'
- 'She's always naughty'
- 'He just can't concentrate on anything'
- 'She'll never have any friends'

The problem with these labels is that they tell children what they *are*. Unfortunately when we tell our children these things they come to believe that they are like this, and so they continue to act in this role.... This is called a self-fulfilling prophecy.

To change a person's behaviour you must *act towards a person as you would like them to be, not as they are*.

Identify a positive alternative to your child's behaviour

Ask yourself, if your child was behaving in ways that you would like them to, what would they be doing *instead* of what is happening now? *These behaviours are the skills that the child needs help to learn.* You can offer this help. For example:

- If your child seems irresponsible, you could help him learn responsibility
- If your child seems selfish, you could help him learn unselfishness
- If your child seems careless, you could help him learn carefulness.

Helping children praise themselves

So-called 'good behaviour' is actually made up of many details. When you use effective praise it is important to draw attention to all the details that you have noticed. Instead of saying something the child has done is 'good'. Look carefully and describe what you see and how it makes you feel. For example:

- 'You got dressed without a fuss and put all the toys into boxes without me asking you. That's called organisation!'
- 'I saw that you were really cross when he took your toy but you didn't hit him, did you. That took real self-control!'
- 'I can see that you've used lots of interesting words in your writing. I like the bit about ... . You must be proud of yourself'.

Actively drawing attention to the positive details in a child's behaviour helps the child to know what he or she can do next time. This helps them to think about themselves in a positive way. And this helps improve behaviour. This is again an example of a self-fulfilling prophecy, but this time it works to the advantage of you and your child!

Setting limits

Your child needs you to be able to firm and set some limits. Sometimes you will need to say 'No' and sometimes you will need to say that you are unhappy about something. In general, however, when you have to say this, spend as little time on it as you possibly can in order to make your point firmly. Then move back quickly to a positive focus.

27 Hitting and kicking, spitting, biting and swearing

It is quite common for young children to go through phases when they deal with their frustrations by hitting, spitting, biting, swearing, or kicking.

These behaviours are often difficult for parents to cope with because they are unpleasant. But more than this, parents become aware that these behaviours make their child unpopular with other children and their parents.

This leaflet looks at these 'anti-social behaviours' in more depth and explains how you can help your child.

Some points to remember

➤ It is essential to try to build a more positive relationship with a child who is beginning to behave in antisocial ways. Without the chance of a positive relationship your child will not want to take the trouble to please you.

➤ Don't be alarmed if your child occasionally hits out or behaves in an antisocial way. You need to be firm with your child that this behaviour is not acceptable. You may need to apologise to the other child or to the child's parent and help your child say sorry too. But don't over-react. Your child is still learning how to manage relationships.

➤ Antisocial behaviour is much more likely if your child is over-tired, ill or hungry or when the family is stressed by difficult events.

➤ Children who more persistently behave in antisocial ways quite often have difficulties in putting their feelings into words. Sometimes they have specific language delays. Does your child need any extra support with these issues?

➤ Remember you are a role model for your child. Make sure your child doesn't see you dealing with anger by hitting or raging. Your child will think that this is a normal and acceptable way to behave.

➤ It takes time and patience to help your child learn to use words to express frustration and feelings. But it is worth persevering!

➤ Once antisocial behaviours have begun they take time to disappear. Even when things are improving there will be occasional bad days. It is important not to overreact to these incidents. Keep focussed on all the positive improvements.

➤ Do ask for professional advice if you are still worried.

Hitting, spitting, biting, swearing, and kicking

Many young children go through phases in which there is some spitting, biting, swearing, kicking or hitting. Because they are all unpleasant and anti-social behaviours, parents often get upset about them. They also get upset because they are embarrassed with other parents and know that these behaviours make their child unpopular with others.

Unfortunately, getting very upset about these behaviours can make them worse. The general tension in the relationships increase, and children can begin to learn that these behaviours trigger a great reaction from their parents, and from other adults and children! Unfortunately, for children who are not getting very much positive attention for other pro-social behaviours, the negative 'telling off' attention can be better than nothing and can make it more likely that the child will repeat the behaviours again.

Understanding antisocial behaviour?

Children tend to behave in antisocial ways for a number of reasons. These include:

➤ Being in situations when they are becoming tense and frustrated but don't have a habit of using words to express their feelings
➤ As a provocation – in situations in which they get little attention for behaving in more appropriate ways
➤ Out of habit, because they have done it before
➤ Copying so as to feel like others that are important to them.

Biting and hitting often happens when young children feel that their space is being invaded or that someone is taking something that they wanted. Spitting and swearing are often forms of attention-seeking or ways of feeling like others. It is important to watch carefully to understand what triggers the behaviour.

How do I help my child?

Children who behave in antisocial ways are often not very popular with others. It can seem that they are just very naughty children. But it is more useful to think of them as children who either don't know how to behave more acceptably or don't want to, because they are feeling alienated within their relationships with others.

It is very difficult to just stop a child's antisocial behaviour. The antisocial behaviours will only stop if the child can learn some different and more socially acceptable ways of dealing with situations. They will also only stop if adults take active steps to build a positive relationship with the child. You can:

➤ Be proactive about building a positive relationship between yourself and your child. Your child needs to know that you like him so that he will want to please you. Children who know that adults care for them have better self-esteem and find self-control much easier.

➤ Be clear that you don't like the antisocial behaviour. But give it as little attention as you can possibly manage. Say 'No' very firmly, deal with the incident and then move quickly on to a positive focus.

➤ Be very proactive about teaching your child socially acceptable ways of resolving disputes and dealing with frustration. You may need to talk through the feelings and show him or her what they can do instead.

28 Playing with your child: helping your child and yourself

Parents are often told that young children need their parents to be firm and consistent. But with many children, particularly those with developmental delays in attention, language and play skills, trying to be firm and consistent isn't enough.

If it seems to the parent that the child is always into trouble and that there are frequent unrewarding battles for control, parents can often feel worn out, exasperated and resentful. In these situations, something may be needed to make the relationship more positive again.

This leaflet explains how regular short periods of child-centred playtime can help your child's development *and* help to develop a more positive relationship between you.

Some points to remember

▲ Some children are more challenging to parent than others. Some children are very active; others react in very intense ways to things. Attention, language and play skills also develop more slowly in some children than in others.

▲ By joining in with your child you can help him or her to develop many skills.

▲ It is very common for parents sometimes to become completely worn out and exasperated with their children, especially if there are other stresses on the family.

▲ Being worn out is often expressed as anger, irritability and impatience towards the child. But irritability can tend to make a child's behaviour worse, so as well as making time for a more positive relationship with your child, you may need to prioritise getting yourself more support or more breaks.

▲ Children *need* positive attention from adults. If you are able to give your child your full positive attention for short periods in the day, your child will gradually become more able to accept that you cannot fit in with them all of the time. He or she will also become more willing to negotiate and co-operate with you when you need to be firm and insist.

▲ It is not helpful to give your child your full attention *all* the time. They can develop an 'addiction' to it and find it difficult to play independently. Independent play is another vital skill.

▲ Remember you *will* need to be firm and insist that your child completes certain activities that he or she doesn't really wish to do on some occasions. Keep these times as short as you can.

▲ If you are still concerned, do ask for professional help.

Why do children need child-led time?

Children *need* attention from their parents. They need to know that their parents are interested in them and will help out when needed. By giving full positive attention to their children, even for short periods parents show their children that they care for and respect them. This is sometimes enough to help the child feel relaxed enough about exploring the world alone sometimes. But the parent can also help develop many of a child's skills during this time.

When children do not have short periods of full positive attention from parents, their development can be affected. They don't have the benefit of the parent's knowledge about the world, but they can often also feel more anxious and uncertain about whether their parent really cares for them. They can be less willing to co-operate.

Children who are not sure about whether their parents have positive feelings for them can also become 'attention-seeking'. They find ways to gain attention through naughty and provocative behaviour that they know will at least get a reaction from adults. Or they may appear to not care about the parent, expressing disinterest or resistance to anything the parent suggests.

Child-led time can therefore help you and your child:

⚠ If you currently have a difficult or strained relationship with your child

⚠ If your child has any delays or difficulties in language, attention, play or in understanding feelings

In a short, child-led play sessions we aim to give our full positive attention to the child, adapting our own behaviour to fit in with what the child is interested in. *During this time, we are not asking the child to fit in with our interests.* Remember that fitting in with adults is very difficult for most young children.

Guidelines for child-led play sessions: Building attachment, attention, language and play skills

The setting

⚠ Find a quiet place to be with your child on a one to one basis.

⚠ Try to make sure that you will not be distracted.

⚠ Make sure you have a range of toys and books suitable for your child's developmental age, not his or her real age.

⚠ Position yourself so that you are at the same level as your child, and so as to make eye contact possible.

The activities

⚠ Let your child choose the activity with you and be prepared to change focus with them if or when he loses interest. (Children learn best from what interests them and this will avoid confrontations with you.)

⚠ Aim to make yourself the most attentive and fun play companion you can be for this short period

⚠ Find ways to join in and gently extend your child's play focus:

– *Extend language and attention skills:* give words for the things that your child is looking at, repeat clearly the sounds and words your child uses, speaking slowly and clearly, use language that is just a bit more advanced than your child's and try not to ask too many questions.

– *Extend play skills* by gently adding new ideas into your child's chosen activity without taking over, by encouraging turn-taking; change focus when your child loses interest

– *Explore feelings and relationships* by listening carefully and talking about them

– *Build your relationship* by smiling a lot, rubbing your child's back, giving hugs, encouraging and praising them and letting him or her know you are enjoying this time with them

⚠ When your child knows that you will sometimes join in with his or her interests, it is usually easier to be firm and insist that he or she sometimes spends 5-10 minutes helping you.

Remember, any time is good for child-led time!

29

Time for your teenager: helping your teenager and yourself

Everyone knows that young children are demanding and need time from their parents. But the situation is more complicated with teenagers. Teenagers usually need to spend more time with children of their own age. But this does not mean that they don't still need opportunities for time with their parents. Indeed, for many teenagers, keeping a positive relationship going with one or more adults who care about them can be one of the most important things that will help them resist some of the greater stresses and challenges of peer pressure.

If your relationship with your teenager is currently difficult there are things you can do to make a difference. This leaflet looks at ways of keeping a positive relationship going with your teenager as he or she makes the transition from childhood to adulthood.

Some points to remember

▲ Some teenagers are more challenging to parent than other teenagers. But all teenagers benefit from a basically positive relationship with their parents wherever possible. This is worth working for. Keep a long view.

▲ One of the best ways to encourage a respectful relationship from your teenager is to model being very respectful of, and a little detached from, the choices that they make about their own lives. Focus on supporting thoughtful decision making rather than laying down do's and don'ts.

▲ Make a point of being interested in what your child is doing and who they are spending time with, without being over-intrusive. Your child will appreciate a quiet awareness from you.

▲ It is very common for parents sometimes to become completely worn out and exasperated with their teenagers. If there are also other stresses on you or the family this makes parenting harder. Being worn out is often expressed as anger, irritability and impatience towards the teenager. But if this starts to happen a lot in a relationship with a teenager it will tend to make the teenager's behaviour worse.

▲ If you are often irritable or impatient you may need to find ways to practise calmness, reduce some of the stresses on yourself and make your own life more interesting and enjoyable. You may also need to urgently try to make your relationship with this teenager more positive.

▲ Simply taking the time to watch a teenager's favourite television programme or video with them from time to time can be a good way of showing that you are happy being with them.

▲ It is not helpful to run round doing everything for your teenager. Your teenager needs to know that though he or she is important to you, you also have other interests and priorities in your life. If you do everything for your child, he or she will not learn these skills. Your teenager will be a more confident and effective adult if they learn to play a part in such things as cooking, housework, and money management.

▲ If you are still worried, do ask for further professional support.

Why do teenagers need time?

Teenagers have a lot to work out. They live between the world of childhood, in which adults were in charge and always knew best, and the world of adults in which they must find their own way. Teenagers often have mixed feelings about this transition period. On the one hand, they may be impatient to be treated as an adult. On the other, they may feel some fear or sadness about not being a small child any more. Teenager behaviour is thus often unpredictable!

Parents have a difficult role to play. Teenagers urgently need adults around to discuss and share things with, but they do not want to be babied and will often, if they feel their parent either 'babies them' or is often unavailable, wish to distance themselves from things that are important to the parents. It may seem sometimes that everything you do seems to be wrong. But it is important to *keep a long view.*

If teenagers don't have a positive relationship with their parents or another adult and feel that they can't discuss things that are bothering them, their peers will have a much greater influence on them. *Teenagers need their parent's involvement.*

Be prepared to learn from your teenager

Difficulties often arise with teenagers when parents either have decided to leave the teenager with too much unsupervised responsibility or when parents have been too confident that they know what their teenagers life is like and how they should behave. It is vital to keep an open mind when listening to teenagers and to be ready to listen and learn from them. *If parents are critical of everything the teenager does, the teenager will not wish to talk.* It is better to say nothing than to lecture and or to criticise frequently.

Making space for teenage time

Teenagers communicate in unexpected moments when they feel it is safe to do so. If you want to keep a good relationship going with your teenager you need to be able to be open, responsive and respectful of *his or her* decision-making abilities, even though you may not agree with everything.

▲ Try to see yourself as a 'consultant' rather than as 'manager'. Regularly say to your child: *'I trust you to make the right decisions for yourself. You know you can ask for my help if you need to.'* Be careful about offering advice unless he or she asks for it. Let them work things out in their own time and way.

▲ Remember your child's self-esteem is still critical:
- Find daily ways to make your affection clear through compliments, appreciation and small gestures,
- Make a point of identifying your teenager's talents and skills and being actively admiring of them

▲ Find ways to help your teenager play genuinely helpful roles in your home. Teenagers grow in confidence when they are given real responsibility.

▲ Your teenager's friendships with others are also critical. Make your home a relaxed or fun place your teenager feels they can easily bring their friends. Encourage your child to bring a friend on family trips or outings.

▲ Make a point of becoming informed about the current favourite crazes, pop music, television programmes or films. Be careful not to put down your child's interests.

▲ Take an active interest in the world around you and find ways to share your interests and enthusiasms and dilemmas with your teenager. They may just listen politely, but they will be taking in more than you realise.

Remember, any moment of the day is good for teenage time!

30 Learning to listen: helping children with their feelings

Conflicts are almost unavoidable in families. One person wants one thing and the other wants something else. In families these conflicts can be resolved by force – who is the person who shouts loudest, sulks most or persists longest? This way of managing conflicts breeds resentment and lets tensions fester and build up.

Another way of managing day-to-day conflicts is to see them as opportunities. Each conflict can be an opportunity to practise some listening and problem-solving skills. Problem-solving in relationships can be learned. It is based on learning respect for others and on an ability to listen carefully.

This leaflet explains more about how to use the skills of listening to feelings and problem-solving in your family.

Some points to remember

▲ Children often have very clear and strong feelings about their experiences. They may not always be able to put these feelings into words without active support from an adult.

▲ Children commonly express their feelings through their play or drawings or behaviour.

▲ Always be respectful of your child's feelings. It is not helpful to tell children that they should or shouldn't feel certain things. Rather than agree or disagree, it is more important to show that you have heard your child's feelings by accurately 'reflecting back' what you have heard.

▲ When children feel that they have been accurately listened to and that their feelings are being taken into account, their behaviour commonly becomes calmer and more mature.

▲ Remember, if you want to encourage your child to talk with you openly, he or she needs to be sure that you will not react with strong anger or disapproval to what they say. This takes practice but you can say, '*I want you to know that I prefer you to tell me than not tell me. I may not always be happy about what you tell me, but I promise not to be cross.' 'If I am worried I may ask you to work something out with me.*'

▲ You can help children to practise their own listening skills when they have to solve conflicts with their siblings and friends.

▲ You can help children learn that listening carefully to their own feelings and to the feelings of others will enable them to know which decisions are good ones.

Which feelings do we have difficulty acknowledging?

Children can often be helped a great deal when adults are able to recognise and acknowledge intense emotions such as anger, rage, fear, terror, hatred, jealousy, shame, sadness, guilt, boredom, disappointment, frustration, tiredness and longing.

Listening accurately doesn't mean allowing all actions

When children know that you have heard them accurately it is often easier to set limits on what they can and cannot do. They are often more open to negotiation. You might need to say for example, *'I can see how angry you are but you mustn't hit when you're angry,'* or *'I can see that you hate doing this homework but it does have to be done. Let's find a way of doing it quickly'.*

Engaging your child's co-operation using listening skills

Children also need to know that *you* also have feelings about things that happen. But they will find it difficult to hear your feelings if they feel you don't listen or if they feel attacked and criticised by you. When you have strong feelings you can:

- ▲ Take the time to talk directly with your child
- ▲ Describe the problem without attacking your child
- ▲ Give your feelings a name
- ▲ Sum up what you wish for, or need, as a parent, briefly without a lecture. *Remember, as a parent you can, and must insist sometimes and set some limits*
- ▲ Be prepared to listen carefully to your child. acknowledge his or her feelings and wishes
- ▲ Work with your child to come up with a mutually acceptable solution.

Parents often don't accept their children's negative feelings

Have you ever heard yourself use any of the following expressions?

- ▲ 'You don't really feel that way ...'
- ▲ 'You're just saying that because ...'
- ▲ 'There's no reason to be so upset'
- ▲ 'You shouldn't say such things about ...'

When we use these expressions with our children, we are automatically denying their feelings. We are effectively telling our children not to trust their own perceptions or judgements but to rely on our own adult judgements instead. We may do this over and over again. When we do this we commonly end up in arguments with our children.

More than this, when we repeatedly tell our children that their perceptions, attitudes or experiences are wrong, they become reluctant to talk to us. But there is an alternative.

Parents can listen to children using empathy

When parents try to listen to their children accurately and non-judgementally, the children become more willing to open up and more confident in them. To do this, children need adults to:

- ▲ Listen with full attention to the words and the feelings
- ▲ Quietly acknowledge the child's feelings, giving them a name. *'It sounds as if you're feeling ...'*
- ▲ Show that they have heard accurately by putting the child's wishes into words. *'It sounds as if you would like ...'*
- ▲ Be careful *not* to criticise or judge the feelings or wishes.

Simply showing a child that you have heard his or her feelings and wishes often helps the child to cope more easily with reality.

Helping siblings get on with each other

Brothers and sisters commonly have strong and mixed feelings about one another. It is quite normal for family members to sometimes hate other members of the family and wish that they were different.

But if your family life is constantly dominated by arguing and fighting between siblings, it is important to know that though you may not be able to prevent all of it, you *can* make a difference and help your children develop a happier relationship between them.

This leaflet offers you some ideas of the ways that you can help.

Some points to remember

▲ Children don't need to be treated equally. They need to know that you love and value them as unique and special in their own right. Each child needs their own protected moments with you.

▲ Make sure that your children have regular periods of quiet time to play together when there is no one else around. Any friendship takes time to build, and siblings often find that others generate emotions and conflicts that are harder to manage.

▲ Make it clear with praise and rewards if necessary how much you enjoy being with your children when they're being pleasant and kind to each other. Let them know that you are sure they are capable of liking each other. And encourage all acts of generosity towards each other

▲ As far as possible, do not take sides or try to solve sibling disputes for them. Help children to learn how to solve their own disputes fairly and take an interest in their problem-solving attempts.

▲ Do not permit children to argue constantly in your presence.

▲ Insist on rules of fairness and safety and basic respectfulness for every family member. For example,
  – No hitting, kicking or hurting
  – No using others things without asking
  – No spoiling others games
  – Apologise for an accident
  – Play fighting only if both are enjoying it
  – Talk don't shout
  – Let everyone have a fair chance to speak etc

▲ For more helpful ideas on this subject, the books *Siblings without Rivalry* and *How to talk so Kids will Listen and Listen so Kids will talk*, both by Adele Faber, are highly recommended.

Conflict and arguments in family life

It is impossible to participate in family life without having some conflicts and arguments. Every family has to cope with these challenges. So when arguments happen, don't dwell on them, move as quickly as possible onto a more positive focus.

In fact, children with siblings have a very good opportunity to learn how to sort out conflicts by negotiation and in a fair way, BUT, your children will only learn these skills if you help them:

The skills to be learned

➤ How to be angry or cross with someone without hitting or hurting them.

➤ How to put feelings into words without shouting and yelling

➤ How to listen carefully and accurately to someone else putting their feelings into words

➤ How to respect other peoples needs as well as their own

➤ How to come up with different solutions to a problem

➤ How to choose solutions that are fair to everyone.

How do children learn these skills?

Children learn conflict resolution skills in a number of ways. They learn by watching you. They learn by experiencing respect and fair solutions to problems, and they learn by practice. It is therefore best to help children practice the process of coming up with solutions to problems. It is not helpful to always get involved in trying to resolve fighting.

How to deal with arguments and fighting

Level One: Low-level bickering

➤ **If possible, ignore it.** Tell yourself your children are having an important experience in conflict resolution

➤ However, if the bickering is dominating the family environment, insist the two that are arguing go into another room until it is sorted out. *It is not helpful to let your children argue constantly in your presence.*

Level Two: Situation heating up – some adult help needed

➤ **Acknowledge their anger:** 'You two sound like you're getting angry with each other'

➤ **Listen carefully and reflect each child's point of view:** 'It sounds to me as if X wants BBC1 and Y wants ITV'

➤ **Describe the problem:** 'That's a tough one to solve. Two wishes and only one television Have you got ideas on what you could do?'

➤ **Express confidence in your children's ability to find their own solution.** 'I'm sure you two can work out something that's fair to you both. I'd like you to go away and sort it out, then come and tell me your solution'.

➤ **Insist they go to sort it out, or leave the room yourself**

Level Three: Situation possibly dangerous

➤ **Enquire** 'Is this a play fight or a real fight'

➤ **Remind them of your house rules:** 'Remember its only play if you both agree. If it's not fun for you both, it must stop'.

Level Four: Situation definitely dangerous – adults needed!

➤ **Describe what you see** 'I see two angry children who are about to hurt each other'

➤ **Separate children** for cooling off period in different rooms

32 Helping temperamentally challenging children

Some children are much harder to parent than others. They test the extreme limits of a parent's patience. Sometimes these temperamental difficulties have been apparent from birth. In other cases the difficulties have emerged gradually perhaps in toddler-hood or perhaps later during the school years. These children can appear insensitive to others, self-centred, provocative and sometimes aggressive. Everyday interactions can appear to involve a battle for control.

This leaflet will look at the needs of temperamentally challenging children and will explain how you can help yourself and your child.

Some points to remember

▲ Temperamentally challenging children are more demanding to parent than other children

▲ If your relationship with a child is difficult, try to think about the following questions:

– has my child always had a difficult temperament?

– when did the difficulties start?

– were there any big stresses on myself, my child or on the wider family at the time the difficulties got worse?

– is my temperament similar or different to my child's?

– what helps? what makes a positive difference?

▲ Temperamentally-challenging children often believe that the world is against them. They don't believe that others like them, but they would like to be liked. So they are very quick to take offence. Keeping a sense of control is very important to them because they think others let them down.

▲ By definition, challenging child find it very hard to take other people's needs into account. They perhaps feel they have not had the experience of other people reliably taking their needs into account at important times when they needed it. To help them learn this skill will take time and determination from you. It is very important to begin to make time to listen at the same time as practising firmness.

▲ Make sure that you find ways to look after your own emotional needs so that when you are with your child you can resist provocation and keep calm and firm about what is or isn't acceptable. Having other interests and pleasures in your spare time can help you keep a useful emotional distance while your child learns that he is cared for and that he can care for others.

▲ Some challenging children can have subtle learning difficulties that have not been fully identified. The child may be really struggling with certain situations. Don't hesitate to ask for further advice or support if you are still worried.

The characteristics of temperamentally challenging children

Temperamentally challenging children usually have a combination of intense temperament traits. For example they:

▲ may react to events with powerful and intense emotions

▲ often have a lot of energy which needs channelling

▲ can be very intelligent, or have some learning difficulties

▲ are often quite insensitive to the needs and feelings of others

When parents are themselves very stretched or stressed in the child's early years, or not very experienced, these basic characteristics can lead to other patterns of behaviour. For example the child may develop:

▲ a desire to do only as they please, acting on impulse alone

▲ a desire to be in control and find ways to control others

▲ a desire to challenge the limits on virtually everything

▲ a reluctance to concentrate on things that 'bore' them.

These children tend to develop a pattern of doing things if they feel like doing them, and not doing them if they don't feel like it. If challenged about their behaviour they become angry and frustrated, resorting to nagging, stone-walling, lies, arguments, tantrums, or aggression. They are ready to believe the world is against them and may take criticism as a personal attack.

Thus an intense pattern of responses in the child in association with stress in the wider family can often lead to behaviour that is very challenging to manage. Temperamentally difficult children are undoubtedly exhausting to parent. Some parents may feel completely helpless and worn down by their child. Others can find themselves in a cycle of never-ending conflicts. This can lead to a tendency to resort, in desperation, to ever harsher attempts at restriction and punishment. *But it is possible to turn things round.*

How do I help my child?

Temperamentally challenging children need extra help from parents in order to *learn* how to make positive relationships with others and how to behave in socially acceptable ways. To learn these skills they need:

A warm attachment with one or more reliable adults

In order to have any influence on your child, it is *essential* to find ways to make your relationship positive. For example:

▲ Find things to praise and encourage on a daily basis

▲ Take an active interest in things that interest your child

▲ Be there regularly when your child needs you

▲ Actively show your affection with gestures and words

▲ Practice the art of staying calm but firm to provocation.

Close supervision

Some children need much closer supervision than others. If you feel your child can often behave in ways that are socially unacceptable or that put him or her or others at risk, you need to make a point of knowing what your child is doing, who they are with and whether they are behaving acceptably.

Consistent rule-based discipline

Some children need very firm consistent and clearly stated rules which are repeated and followed through on again and again as long as is necessary. Rule-based discipline must always be alongside close supervision and *affection.*

Practice in negotiation of problems with discussion

Impulsive difficult children need practice in negotiating agreements to conflicts using reason and words. As a child you can help your child learn to listen by listening carefully yourself, and by helping them express feelings and views.

33 Helping children with fears and anxiety

Many children and adults suffer from anxiety at some point or in some area of their lives. Anxiety is quite normal. It only becomes a problem when it starts to control our decisions and prevents us from doing positive things that will help us develop and become more self-confident.

If anxiety is starting to be a problem for you or your child, it is important for you to know that anxiety can be overcome. It is not necessary to live with it for ever. It is possible, for example, to learn the key skills of self-understanding, relaxation and positive self-talk. With these skills you can overcome a difficult past and do whatever you want!

This leaflet explains about anxiety and about how you can help yourself or your child.

Positive self-talk and relaxation

Self-talk and practice with relaxation skills can be very helpful if a child is feeling anxious about doing something. You can help them learn to say these things to themselves:

Preparation for a difficult situation

▲ 'I'm feeling anxious, but that's OK.'

▲ 'I'll take a deep breath and relax inside, I can handle this.'

▲ 'If I do get worrying sensations, that's normal, they won't last long.'

▲ 'It's not going to be as bad as I think.'

▲ 'I've coped with difficult things before.'

▲ 'I might enjoy it if I try.'

▲ 'Avoiding the problem will make it worse. I know I can do it!'

Coping in the difficult situation

▲ 'Float don't fight. This will soon be behind me. I'm doing well!'

▲ 'These sensations are just anxiety; I know they can't harm me.'

▲ 'Relax. Think calming thoughts. These feelings will go away.'

▲ 'In facing up to my anxiety, I'm not letting it restrict me.'

▲ 'Be calm, concentrate on what I'm doing.'

▲ 'One step at a time, slowly does it.'

Praise following success in coping

▲ 'Great! Well done me! I coped!'

▲ 'I'm getting better. I'm in control.'

▲ 'I did that really well.'

▲ 'I handled it; it will be easier next time.'

▲ 'Small steps gradually add up to big progress!'

Remember, anxious children often have anxious parents. You can help your child by sharing with them your own steps to become more confident in your own life. Talk with them about your own successes. You might say: *'Not long ago, I couldn't do 'X' but now I can and I'm really proud of myself. I decided not to let anxiety beat me!'*

Don't hesitate to ask for professional advice if you are still concerned.

Why do we feel anxious?

Children and adults feel anxious when they feel unsafe or not in control. They can worry:

➤ that something dangerous will happen that will harm them or someone that they care about

➤ that they will make a mistake or not be able to do something

➤ that other people will be critical or will reject them

➤ that they will lose control

Young children show that they are feeling anxious through their behaviour. They often do this by clinging, crying or general irritability. Sometimes they complain of tummy aches or sickness. Parents can often worry themselves if they are not sure how to help.

What happens in the body when we feel anxious?

When we feel anxious our bodies become tense. Sometimes this increased tension is shown in sleep difficulties or loss of appetite or constant worrying. These symptoms make it difficult to concentrate on other things. They can be exhausting. This is called 'generalised anxiety'.

Sometimes the symptoms of anxiety come on very suddenly and unexpectedly – our hearts beat faster, our breathing becomes shallower, we may start to sweat, our stomachs can churn or we may think we are about to faint. This is called a 'panic attack' and it can be very frightening. People often think something must be seriously wrong with them, and become worried it may happen again. When the anxiety symptoms arise in relation to one specific thing, such as school or dogs or spiders we call it a 'phobia'.

Can anxiety harm us?

The main way in which anxiety can harm us is that it can stop us doing things that we may enjoy or which may help us to develop further. Anxiety can often make us more isolated. It can cause us to avoid things. When people worry a lot of the time, the anxiety and isolation can become mixed up with depression.

Overcoming anxiety

It is not wrong to feel anxious. Most anxious people have had some past of experiences that have been very difficult for them. The anxiety they feel is usually understandable in relation to these past experiences. However it is important to decide whether the anxiety is helpful or unhelpful in the circumstances of the present.

People who let anxiety dominate their lives – worrying about all the awful things that could possibly happen, or what others will think – often find that their self-confidence gradually gets weaker and weaker.

The more a person avoids situations, the less opportunity they have to find ways of coping with challenges, and gaining confidence.

First small steps

We can only overcome anxiety by trying things out and being successful and by finding out that our worst fears haven't happened. We make progress with small steps. So you can help your child to:

➤ Begin to become aware of his or her own pattern of anxiety symptoms and to become curious about them. When do they increase? And when do they decrease?

➤ Help them to feel that anxiety is OK and that you will support them. But be positive and confident that it can and *will* pass.

➤ Help them identify the times when they are not affected by anxiety? What is different about these situations?

➤ Help your child to identify a small step that would represent progress. Make sure that that the challenge is as small as it needs to be to make success possible. Don't be tempted to rush.

➤ Praise and encourage all your child's steps at overcoming anxiety and at using positive self-talk.

As you overcome anxiety, confidence grows!

34 Helping children with jealousy

Jealousy is a painful and rather unacceptable emotion linked to insecurity that is nonetheless at the root of much tension and conflict within family situations.

Children's jealousy can be triggered off very easily by competition for adult attention. This can be particularly likely if the parents are themselves feeling very stressed and under-supported at an important stage of the child's development. Sometimes parents really do struggle to have enough time to go round. But the behaviour of a jealous child can be very challenging as it is often very demanding and associated with other emotions such as anxiety, resentment, irritability and depression.

This leaflet explains about jealousy and about how you can help your child.

Some points to remember

▲ The most important time to be careful about triggering feelings of jealousy is when your children are young. In particular take care on the arrival of a new baby, step-siblings or new partners. Ensure that your child's world is not changed too much, that they don't feel abandoned and that they are not suddenly expected to be much more grown up.

▲ Remember once your child has developed a tendency towards jealousy, these insecurities rarely go away completely. They are very easy to trigger off and so the symptoms may become more apparent again when there are new stresses in the family or when your child is very tired or worried about other things.

▲ If the situation seems to have got worse again after a good patch, try to think if there have been other pressures on your child or family. Are there any ways in which you could relieve some pressure?

▲ Try to make at least some one: one time available for each of your children. A 10 min listen to them before they go to sleep helps every child.

▲ Wherever possible help your children learn to resolve their own disagreements. If you get involved you will inevitably end up taking sides leaving one child feeling resentful. Children need to feel that they are considered unique and special to their parents. They don't need the same treatment but they do need to feel that parents are being fair.

▲ Though it is helpful to try to understand your child's jealous behaviour, it is not helpful to let them behave in socially unacceptable ways. They may need more patience from you as they learn to deal with their emotions differently.

▲ If you are still worried, don't hesitate to ask for further support or advice.

Why do children experience jealousy?

Children experience jealousy when they feel anxious about the availability of love and attention from the adults or friends who are most important to them. Jealousy is therefore a complex emotion. For example children may feel:

➤ Let down by and upset by a parent or friend they had cared for – it may seem to them that this parent has chosen a sibling, for example, in preference to them

➤ Resentful and angry in relation to the preferred child

➤ Bad about having jealous feelings

➤ Hyper-vigilant to apparently trivial details in social situations that might hint at unfairness or rejection.

➤ Anxious about doing something that may cause them to be rejected or abandoned again

➤ Doubtful about their own self-worth

➤ Full of feelings of rage and aggression towards the parent/friend

How do children behave when they experience jealousy?

Because jealousy involves such complicated emotions, children with a tendency towards jealousy can be difficult and unpredictable in their behaviour. They may be more sensitive at some times than at others. They may express their feelings through demanding and attention-seeking behaviour, rages, passive-aggressive behaviour or sometimes by withdrawal and sulks or depression. The challenging behaviour can be directed towards the parent/friend or towards the rival.

So almost by definition, children who experience jealousy also have a quite fragile sense of self-esteem and self-confidence that can easily be affected by being in situations where they feel they are in competition with someone that they feel the parent/friend may like better. Parents need to be very careful not to fall into a vicious circle with a jealous child by misinterpreting their difficult behaviour simply as deliberate naughtiness.

Avoiding jealousy

Jealousy is very commonly triggered by the arrival of a new baby or person in the family, particularly if the child is at an age or stage when they are needing a lot of adult attention. What the child is sensitive to is, 'Has my parent or friend got less time and affection for me than they used to have?' Steps can be taken to reassure a child about transition.

Before the change

➤ Talk to your child about the change and involve him or her in thinking about it. This can include talking about what will change and what won't change, and what welcome to give the new arrival.

After the change

➤ Make sure to keep some familiar routines and special one:one times going with the child.

➤ Actively take gentle steps to build a relationship between the child and the new arrival. Support, encourage and praise all nurturing and kindness. 'You were so helpful to me'

➤ Take steps to point out to the child how much the new arrival likes them. '*Did you see how she smiled at you?*'

➤ Make time to listen when the child has times of wishing the new arrival would go away.

Steps to take when jealousy and anxiety already exist

➤ Observe the jealousy but don't comment too much on it.

➤ Think about what might have happened at the time the jealousy first started and about how the child might have experienced events at the time?

➤ Ask yourself when the jealousy tends to show itself most. Are there any other pressures that make it worse? Can you help?

➤ Make sure you have enough positive one-to-one time with the sensitive child

➤ Help your child have some time to talk about their feelings

➤ Take active steps to help your child develop a positive relationship with the person they are typically most jealous of

➤ Help your child to build his or her own skills and independent areas of success.

35 Coping with irritability, sulking and a quick temper

Most people get angry from time to time. Anger is an important and very powerful emotion that gives us clues about our own current well-being and about what we feel strongly about. But it sometimes happens that a person is frequently irritable or is getting angry very quickly and very often.

These frequent angry explosions can be a problem because they can be so destructive. Property can be damaged, but more importantly relationships can be damaged. People do and say things to each other when they are angry that can cause real hurt or harm. Trust gets damaged.

This leaflet explains about anger and about how you can help yourself or your child.

Some points to remember

▲ Anger is a healthy and important emotion. But is not helpful for children or adults to be allowed to get their own way by being irritable, aggressive, with tantrums or with sulks. This is a form of intimidation and allows them to behave as a **bully**.

▲ Angry people often like to blame others. They are often very poor at taking responsibility for their own actions or taking care of their own needs. Taking responsibility is hard work and takes practice.

▲ If your child has recently begun to become more irritable and angry, take some time to think through why your child may be feeling more upset or stressed. Remember children often express anger if they can't yet put their feelings into words. Try to listen and see if you can help by releasing some pressure.

▲ Children find it hard to live with irritable parents. They may respond with irritable and unco-operative behaviour. Parents need patience to be able to defuse situations in families. If you are often irritable, make it a priority to work out how to help yourself become less stressed.

▲ Make it very clear that anger and frustration must NOT be expressed by hitting you or others, and that broken objects must be replaced

▲ Work out some ways of calming things down. Many people find that when they are getting angry they need to go somewhere to cool off. Others find that they can take a deep breath and count to ten.

▲ When – and only when – the situation is calmer, try to get the feelings expressed in words. Help your child to say what they were feeling and why, and what they would like. Help them listen carefully to you too.

▲ Always praise your child (or yourself) when you notice them coping with challenging situations in a more mature way.

▲ If you are still concerned, don't hesitate to ask for professional help.

Why do people get angry or sulk?

People get angry when they feel upset, frustrated, criticised or put upon:

Angry people often struggle to put feelings into words while remaining calm: They may feel:

- ⋗ Upset that things aren't going the way they want them to
- ⋗ Sensitive about something
- ⋗ Hurt or defensive in relation to criticism
- ⋗ Annoyed at the sense that others are making Unreasonable demands on them
- ⋗ It may have become a habit to bully others with their anger
- ⋗ Exhausted and unable to cope because of multiple pressures.

It is OK to be angry but it is not OK to hurt or bully others when we are angry. We must learn to put our feelings and wishes into words in ways that help ourselves and others.

What happens in the body when we get angry?

Anger and frustration are high-tension emotions in the body. When they are not expressed, the body can feel like a taut elastic band, ready to snap at any moment. Our muscles are tight. Our concentration is focused and we are hyper-sensitive to other challenges from any direction. Angry tension can build until we are not able to keep it under control any more. And then it usually finds an outlet.

Sometimes however people feel they must not express their anger and so they try to hold on to it. Children often find it very difficult to put their feelings into words. Unexpressed high tension feelings can comes out in general irritability, or in regular flare-ups or tantrums. It may come out in much more subtle ways of being unco-operative. Or it may be let on on someone weaker who can't, or won't, fight back. Feelings of unexpressed frustration and tension can sometimes be behind symptoms of depression.

Helping a child or adult who often gets angry or sulks

Stop and step back

It is not helpful or possible to try to reason or negotiate with someone who is in a rage or having a tantrum. Next time you or your child gets angry or begins sulking, insist they calm down before they speak to you or others or insist on a break. Ask your child to leave the room or leave the room yourself. Try to avoid talking with them until they are able to speak calmly and reasonably.

Think and talk

Put feelings and wishes into words. If a child or adult is feeling upset and angry it is very important that they learn to put their feelings and wishes into words in a calm and civil way, and in a way that doesn't attack others. This is the skill of **assertiveness.**

Try to help your child work out what thoughts and feelings were happening in the immediate situation that triggered the rage, tantrum or sulk. Encourage them to put their feelings thoughts and wishes into words. Listen carefully and calmly.

Trigger ⟶ thoughts and feelings ⟶ wishes

Listen and learn

Practice listening and negotiating with others. When the child or adult has had a chance to express themselves in a more calm and civil way, ask them to listen carefully to your feelings and wishes. Explain that you will do your best to help if you can but that you and others do have some limits. Help them to work out a solution that is acceptable to all parties. Encourage the child or adult to apologise for his or her unacceptable behaviour, then forgive them and move on.

36 Helping children and adults with depression

Many people have times in their lives when they feel down and a bit low. However, sometimes these feelings are difficult to throw off. The symptoms can remain with a person for weeks or even months. When these ordinary feelings have become more persistent they can seriously interfere with the person's ability to enjoy life. The person may be suffering from depression.

It is not always easy for parents to know what to look for and how to help children with depression. However, it *is* important to try to offer support to a child who is depressed.

This leaflet will explain about depression and its symptoms and about how you can help yourself or your child.

Some points to remember

▲ It is better to act as early as possible in the treatment of depression. If you suspect depression, be proactive, and seek help early.

▲ Some people find that medication can help get them through a difficult patch by lifting their mood enough to help them feel able to carry on. But medication only treats the symptoms. On its own medication is rarely enough.

▲ It is important to give depressed children and adults a chance to talk. But listening is not enough. If you are not careful you will contribute to the person's depression by letting them simply rehearse their negative feelings and thinking patterns.

▲ Grief and mourning can be a healthy form of depression related to a period of adjustment. Giving people time to grieve is important.

▲ Effective therapy for persistent depression always involves helping a person learn some new thinking patterns. If you can help a depressed person identify any realistic wishes, and can help them work out some small steps towards achieving their goals. This will increase their sense of hope and mastery.

▲ Depressed people need help in keeping activities going and in building and maintaining a social network of peers and supportive adults outside the family. Gentle exercise is particularly important. They may be quite resistant to it, but it is out of activity that new possibilities can emerge.

▲ Depression can take time to lift. But it is worth persevering. Depression of any sort can be an opportunity for a person to take to take a deep look at their own experience, feelings, thinking and deepest wishes, and make some important changes. People who come through depression often have a much better understanding of themselves and others.

Why do people become depressed?

Children and adults can become depressed when they look towards the future and experience a sense of helplessness and hopelessness.

Depression can be related to major losses and/or to a major sense of failure or entrapment. The person may feel:

▲ that they cannot control things that are important to them

▲ That whatever they do will not make any difference

▲ That they have tried and failed and cannot change things

▲ That whatever they do will not be right

▲ Anxious, guilty and/or shamed

▲ Exhausted and burned out

Depressed people commonly hold very negative views about their own Self, about the world and about their own future. These negative thoughts often go round and round. Depressed people commonly have a sense of failure in relation to something important and a conviction that as a consequence they are worthless and that others don't and will never like them as they really are.

What happens in the body when we are depressed?

Depression is a slowed down feeling – a sensation of heaviness and weight. Some of the common symptoms of depression include tearfulness, irritability, sleeplessness, negative or suicidal thinking, feelings of tiredness, loss of appetite, lack of interest and motivation, loss of ability to concentrate and withdrawal from social activities.

Depression can sometimes be triggered by biological problems such as thyroid imbalances, physical inactivity or the patterns associated with the female hormonal cycles. Some people seem to be sensitive to light, and some families appear to have vulnerabilities to the onset of depression following stress. Very commonly however, depression tends to set in after a long period of living with a high tension emotion such as **anxiety or anger**. The depression tells us that the person is now feeling helpless and hopeless.

Helping depressed children and adults

Most depressed people have had a history of experiences that have been very difficult for them. They are commonly courageous people who feel they have tried everything they could. But when depression becomes established it is a form of illness in which the person begins to think in ways that distort reality and contribute to them feeling even more helpless and hopeless. Depressed people tend to have very fixed ideas, see things in black and white terms, always imagine the worst and often take responsibility for everything bad that happens. Once established, depression takes time to shift. In order to help:

▲ The child/adult needs someone to make time to *listen* and to try to understand how they have been experiencing events in their world. This listening offers a chance to explore why the person may have feelings of helplessness and hopelessness? *But* listening is not enough.

▲ The child or adult needs help in putting their deepest wishes into words, and help in working out whether these wishes are *realistic*.
  – If their wishes are not realistic, then it is important to help them come to terms with the feelings of sadness, and disappointment involved in letting go of these wishes and hopes. This is an experience of grief and mourning. Grieving always takes time.
  – If their wishes (or some of them) are realistic then it is important to help them to identify small steps or achieveable goals to work towards, so that they can regain a sense of hope and mastery.

▲ The child or adult needs help in identifying and challenging the distorted negative thinking patterns that are part of a depressive illness. They need support and practice in learning to think positively and realistically about themselves, others and their future.

▲ The child/adult must be helped to maintain physical and social activities. They often want to do less and less. However, it is very important to gently but firmly insist they do something as it is through activity that new possibilities emerge. You may need to join in with them.

37 Understanding guilt and shame

Guilt and shame are very difficult emotions to talk about and yet many children and adults with long-standing mental health difficulties struggle with these feelings more than any other. Guilt and shame can be important emotions that are part of healthy relationships. They remind us that other people exist, that they have needs that we must consider, and that we sometimes make mistakes.

However guilt and shame can exist in a *toxic* form associated with intense discomfort or anxiety. In this form, they can overwhelm a person and threaten to prevent them from acting positively. Toxic guilt and shame make a person feel unworthy, exposed, useless, bad and unhappy to their core. As these feelings are so unpleasant a means of escape from awareness is often sought via various forms of blocking such as activity, drugs or alcohol. When escape is no longer possible, depression may set in.

There are no easy methods to overcome toxic guilt and shame. But it is possible. This leaflet may help you to begin thinking about what you can do to help yourself or your child.

Some points to remember

▶ *Many people live in the shadow of toxic guilt and shame, but as these feelings are very hard to live with, and hard to talk about, people often try to avoid awareness of them.*

▲ It is impossible to overcome toxic guilt and shame without help from others. To make progress it is necessary to ask for help. Help is needed from someone who will not be judgemental.

▲ To heal toxic guilt and shame, the person usually has to begin a process of learning to love, trust and accept their own self with greater unconditionality, that is, without reference to what they do and have done. This often involves learning to reduce demands for perfection, and includes forgiveness of self and others. It often involves having to face the pain and discomfort of talking openly about experiences that may have been unbearably difficult. It is essential to find a trustworthy and reliable person to do this with.

▲ Talking about and exploring experiences with others who are not judgemental allows the person to begin to understand the full range of their true feelings about the things that happened, as well (and this is often the most difficult) their beliefs about their own part in these unhappy events. Over time this process can put the person back in touch with a more confident self and eventually helps them to make more understanding contact with others.

▲ But *talking and exploring are not enough.* It is also necessary to learn some new skills. This can include such things as self-care, assertiveness, more helpful forms of self-talk, and practical ways of dealing with critical and shaming others. Parents may want to work on their own parenting skills.

▲ Remember to help a shame-prone child; you may have to start by doing a lot of work with yourself. Shame-proneness often runs in families. Most people who decide to do this work find it very challenging but very worthwhile in the long run.

Basic trust, healthy guilt and healthy shame

Young children are totally dependant on their carers. In the course of healthy development in the very early years of life, children develop a confidence or basic trust that their carers will respond to them positively when they need help. They enjoy the positive relationship with the adult.

The feelings of healthy guilt and shame are thus based on important dependency relationships. They come into play gradually during childhood, from two to three years of age. They can be seen when a child is away from the adult and thinking of doing something that they know the important adult would disapprove of. Healthy guilt and shame can provide breaks to self-centred behaviour. They can be the feelings linked to the important relationship that remind the child to think of others and of longer-term consequences. Healthy guilt and shame are linked to specific behaviours and are short-lived feelings that are a critical part of the ways in which human beings learn to live in peaceful social groups.

The important thing about healthy guilt and healthy shame is that it is part of a *supportive* relationship between a child and an adult, which allows for the legitimate needs of the child. The child knows that he or she can restore positive feelings into their relationship with the adults or others that they depend on. They know how to repair the important relationship. They know that if mistakes happen that they will be forgiven and that the bond is not broken. Essentially, the child feels safe in the relationship.

In contrast, Toxic guilt and shame are more all encompassing feelings, related to whole areas of behaviour or worse to a sense that the person's whole self is somehow disapproved of or not cared for or not worthy in the eyes of one or more important attachment figures. The guilt and shame are felt by the individual but are part of a relationship in which a person feels much *judged* by one or more others. Guilt and shame may arise when a person comes to believe that asking for support with their own needs is not legitimate, and will not be fully supported.

Toxic guilt and toxic shame

So, toxic guilt and shame can arise when a child or adult comes to believe that they have permanently lost (or are at risk of permanently losing) the approval of people that they care about or depend on. The sufferer believes that he or she has been 'abandoned' (or will be abandoned) by an important person (or sometimes by God) because of something that they have done, or not done, or needed. A child or adult with these experiences typically feels very anxious, unsafe but also, sometimes, as they begin to question their own experiences, resentful in the relationship(s).

Another aspect of toxic guilt and shame is that children and adults also feel very unsafe with *themselves*, because they have come to believe (as a result, perhaps, of what they have been told) that *they* are somehow fully responsible for the situation they are in. There is no escape from the self who is not approved of, liked or trusted.

Toxic guilt and shame are extremely difficult feelings to live with. Consequently, people may try a range of methods to block awareness of the feelings. For example:

▲ Defiant coping – the person may cope by actively denying *any* responsibility for a difficult situation or by denying any feelings of neediness. People who cope with the discomfort of having needs or making errors often appear very defensive, self-contained and ready to blame others.

▲ Anxious coping – the person copes by accepting far too much responsibility and by trying to second guess others responses. They typically try hard to be very good to avoid being shamed further.

When feelings associated with toxic guilt and shame become intensified, perhaps as a result of new life events, a person's coping mechanisms may start to break down. Individuals may resort to intense activity, drugs or alcohol to escape awareness. When this is impossible they may lapse into states of helplessness and deep depression.

38 Could my child have an Autistic Spectrum Disorder, and how can I help?

The terms 'autism', 'autistic spectrum disorder', or 'Aspergers Syndrome', tend to be used when a child appears to be having above average difficulties in understanding the social world of relationships with other people.

Children with autism or Asperger's Syndrome are not all identical. The difficulties in understanding the social world are sometimes mild and sometimes more severe. It is important to detect these difficulties as early as possible, because when we know that a child has these difficulties we can be more sympathetic to their behaviours and we can offer them the right sort of help.

This leaflet will look at the area of autism in more depth and will explain how you can help your child.

Some points to remember

▲ No two children with an autistic spectrum disorder are the same. There is reason to be concerned if at the age of 18 months your child has some unusual behaviours, makes little eye contact, and/or doesn't show you things or look at things you point out to him/her.

▲ Autism is understood to be a life-long condition. However children with autistic spectrum difficulties can be helped considerably, if their difficulties are recognised as early as possible and the right supportive help is offered. There are growing numbers of children who were once diagnosed with autism, who no longer have any autistic traits.

▲ All children with autism struggle to understand the world and are therefore often quickly overwhelmed by it.

▲ Parents and other immediate carers of the child are in the best position to help the young child who has suspected autistic difficulties because they spend most time with the child.

▲ It is difficult to say exactly what help or provision a child with an autistic spectrum disorder will need in terms of schooling or in later adulthood. Some children manage in mainstream schools with support, others are happier in special or residential schools. Some adults can live independent lives and others need much more support.

▲ Children with autism are very challenging to parent and can have an impact on the whole family. It is very important to remember that everyone's needs must be taken into account. Some compromising is usually essential.

▲ Many families gain a lot of support through talking with other families who have experienced similar challenges. Useful organisations include the National Autistic Society and Contact a Family.

What is an autistic spectrum disorder?

The term 'autistic spectrum disorder' tends to be used when we observe that a child is having significant difficulties, delays or unusual features in the following areas:

▲ *Social relationships:* Children with autism commonly appear less interested in others. From a very early age, they commonly make less eye contact and may approach others less to show or point things out. They may prefer to play alone and show little imaginative play in their earliest years. Forming friendships is hard for them though they may get on well with, and show great affection towards, one or two trusted and familiar children or adults.

▲ *Language and communication* Some children with autism never learn to speak; Many others learn to speak later than average children and this may be in slightly odd or stereotyped ways, sometimes showing a preoccupation with certain subjects.

▲ *Unusual interests, activities or behaviours.* Children with autism tend to like routines and familiarity. They can become distressed if routines are interrupted. They may take an intense interest in particular objects, topics or activities involving the repetition of particular patterns, affecting sight, taste, smell, hearing or other body movements. Some children in addition to their difficulties have areas of special talents in drawing, music or maths.

The origins of autistic spectrum difficulties are complex and not yet fully understood. Many children on the spectrum have sensory difficulties and become quickly overloaded.

Sometimes the difficulties seem to run in families in association with other language-based difficulties. Sometimes there are other difficulties. The difficulties usually become apparent before the child is three years old and boys are affected much more commonly. The term 'Asperger's Syndrome' is reserved for children with good language skills but poor social understanding. Autism is not caused by bad parenting.

How can I help my child?

Children with autism need active help as early as possible to overcome and/or minimise their difficulties. Like most people, they thrive best in supportive environments that emphasise the gradual building up of their skills.

▲ Seek advice from professionals and other parents and an early diagnosis if possible.

▲ Consider any sensitivities that may distress your child or exaggerate their difficulties for example to diet, certain noises or sensations

▲ Simplify your child's learning environment so that they don't get so easily overwhelmed. Many children with autism are helped by having a lot of 1:1 time with supportive adults or children in a quiet space

▲ Encourage social interaction and communication skills All children communicate, the trick is to work out what your child does currently understand, and how they currently communicate in order to build on these skills. Gestures, photos and games can all nurture your child's interest in communicating with you. Children with autism can become very loving and social

▲ Build alternative behaviours to reduce unusual behaviours. You cannot simply stop unusual behaviours. It is therefore essential to build up your child's alternative skills and interests. You can often build a first bridge to a very isolated child by 'joining in' with their favourite behaviours and then gently interesting them in your world. This can be a task involving great stamina and patience. It cannot easily be done without support from others.

▲ Enjoy and support your child for the unique person they are. Children with autism are very sensitive to the attitudes of people around them. One important step to helping your child is the basic step of really appreciating them as they are right now.

39

Could my child have Attention Deficit Hyperactivity Disorder (ADHD), and how can I help?

The term 'Attention Deficit Hyperactivity Disorder' tends to be used when a child shows persistent signs of over-activity, difficulties in attending to things and impulsiveness. For this term to be used, these symptoms usually have to be experienced as a problem in more than one setting.

It is easy to confuse ADHD with normal growing up or with other learning difficulties. Many children, especially young boys are very active and rather distractible or inattentive. Their behaviour is consequently more challenging to handle.

However active children with attention difficulties can be helped. This leaflet looks at ADHD in more depth and explain how you can help your child.

Some points to remember

⚠ Young children are naturally very active and on the go. They naturally have a short attention span and high levels of energy that needs channelling. In most children, the natural processes of brain maturation eventually come to play a restraining influence on the young child's natural activity levels and distractibility.

⚠ Active children need parents with very good parenting skills. Parents need to provide a positive but firm atmosphere and a lot of supervision to make sure that their children stay out of trouble. The short attention child needs extra help to 'learn to be good'.

⚠ Active children *cannot* just sit still when they are no longer interested. They tolerate boredom very badly. It is therefore important to have a range of interesting activities available.

⚠ Children with poor attention skills are very sensitive to high stress environments. Their behaviour can become even more difficult to handle. It is therefore vital to work for as much calmness around them as possible at home and at school. If your child's behaviour is becoming more difficult, see if you can identify any current stresses on your child. Are there ways to relieve these stresses?

⚠ Listening and talking as much as possible with your child in calm settings, will help extend their attention span and keep a good relationship going between you.

⚠ Provide extra help in getting organised and in finding ways to remember things. Routines and regular reminders will all help.

⚠ Medication does appear to have a calming effect on some children, but does not help every child, and there can be side effects. If the symptoms are found to be a serious problem in home and in school you could discuss the possibilities with your Doctor or Paediatrician.

What is ADHD?

The term Attention Deficit Hyperactivity Disorder tends to be used when a child shows persistent symptoms of:

▲ *High levels of activity* including constant restlessness, fidgeting, or moving about

▲ *Attention difficulties* including forgetfulness, disorganisation, and difficulties concentrating

▲ *Impulsiveness* including interrupting conversations, and acting without thinking

There is a lot of controversy about the diagnosis of ADHD. ADHD is much more common in boys than in girls, but boys generally show a need for much more physical motor activity. Girls generally begin to concentrate on table-top activities for example, at a much younger age than boys. Some people therefore feel that ADHD describes the extreme end of boy's normal patterns of behaviour. Some children appear to have attention difficulties without hyperactivity. This is usually referred to as ADD. It is more common in girls. ADHD is not usually formally diagnosed before a child is 7 years old.

Parenting very active children

Whether or not you feel that the diagnosis of ADHD is appropriate for your child, it is clear that parenting very active children is extremely demanding and exhausting. It can seem that the child is never behaving appropriately and is constantly getting into trouble. This is hard for the child and hard for the parent.

Parents often feel frustrated and embarrassed by their child's behaviour and can worry that their child's difficulties are their fault or that others will *think* that their child's behaviour is their fault. *ADHD or active behaviour is not caused by bad parenting.*

How do I help my child and myself?

Active children with poor attention skills cannot, by definition, attend to one thing for very long. They are often forgetful and distractible. It is important to realise that you cannot improve a child's attention skills by getting cross with them. There are however several steps you can take: These include:

▲ Accept the fact that your child is an active child. It is not his fault; it is not your fault. He or she is not being deliberately naughty, but he will need much more help from you 'to learn to be good'

▲ Remember that attention skills and calm behaviour are things that *develop* gradually in children.

▲ Remember, active children are often in trouble with adults so you will need to work very hard to keep your relationship positive with your child. Use praise and encouragement wherever you can. Try to make a point of praising concentration and self-control whenever you see it.

▲ Remember, active children need very regular changes of activity. They also need plenty of time for out-door play, and can be greatly helped by involvement in sports and physical activities requiring some concentration

▲ Children with poor attention skills often have weak skills in language and independent play. You can help your child develop these skills by having a daily half-an-hour of one to one play with them in which you let them take the lead. Your child may find playing with one other calm child easier than being in a group situation.

▲ Symptoms of over-activity, forgetfulness and irritability are often made worse by tiredness, illness and hunger. Try to make sure that your child has a regular routine for meals and bed-times. Some children are sensitive to diet.

▲ Very active children need *very* firm handling of their behaviour. You need to speak to them directly to make sure that they are listening and you need to be able to insist that they do as you ask in some situations.

40 Could my child have developmental dyspraxia, and how can I help?

The term developmental dyspraxia tends to be used whenever a child appears to be having above average difficulties in the co-ordination of gross motor and fine motor movements, often with other perceptual and/or language related difficulties.

In the past, people may have thought of dyspraxic children as 'clumsy and/or careless.' Such labels can have a very damaging effect on children's self-esteem especially when they may be trying their very hardest to be careful. Now we know that the difficulties in co-ordination can be very real. We also know that, with the right help, these difficulties can be gradually overcome.

This leaflet looks at dyspraxia in more depth and explains how you can help your child.

Some points to remember

▲ No two children with dyspraxia are exactly the same.

▲ Children with dyspraxia can be helped if their difficulties are recognised (as early as possible) and if they are given the right sort of support and encouragement in school and at home.

▲ If your child appears to be clumsy or careless, be careful not to criticise them harshly. Discuss the issue with your child. What do they think about it? They may really be glad of some specific help to try to overcome their difficulties.

▲ Dyspraxic difficulties can often be made worse by tiredness, illness, stress or anxiety. If the problems seem to be getting worse, have a think about what else is going on. Are there ways to relieve some pressure on your child?

▲ Children with dyspraxic difficulties may seem to avoid activities that they find difficult. This is not helpful, as nothing can be learned by avoidance. You can help your child by being firm about the need to persevere with at least some of the activities that they are finding difficult. Use lots of praise and encouragement! Make sure that the level is right so your child always experiences success.

▲ When children with significant dyspraxic problems don't have the right support and encouragement, they can have a significantly higher risk of developing major behavioural problems. This is good reason to get help as soon as you can!

▲ Always discuss your concerns with your child's teachers or contact your local Occupational Therapy Department. They will be able to offer additional advice.

What is dyspraxia?

Dyspraxia is best thought of as a disorder associated with an immature development of the brain, particularly evident around the co-ordination of movements. The difficulties may include things such as:

▲ Irritability and/or feeding or sleep difficulties as an infant

▲ High levels of motor activity, constant movement, shrill voice

▲ 'Clumsiness', falling, bumping into objects, messy eating

▲ Sensitivity to noise, textures on clothing

▲ Very brief or absent crawling phase, no clear handedness

▲ Toe-walking, difficulties with balance, running, and/or bikes

▲ Delayed language development, poor articulation

▲ Avoidance of jigsaws or constructional toys

▲ Trouble with dressing, shoe laces, physical exercise

▲ Disorganised use of page in drawings, or when handwriting

▲ Limited concentration skills, problems following instructions

▲ A mismatch between intellectual abilities and performance

▲ Avoidance of writing or putting ideas on paper, seen as lazy

▲ Tendency to social isolation, often with behaviour problems

▲ Easily distressed, emotional, ongoing tantrums.

Children with dyspraxia do not necessarily have all of these difficulties. The difficulties can be mild or more severe. The difficulties are more commonly found amongst boys.

What happens to the child with dyspraxia?

The main difficulty for a child with dyspraxic difficulties is that they do not make easy progress with many of the tasks required in the school environment. This can be a source of great frustration to them and many children can become hyper-sensitive to their failures preferring not to participate than try and fail. They can easily become switched off from learning.

Helping your child

If you suspect that your child many be having real difficulties with these dyspraxic types of problems, it is very important to take them seriously and give your child extra support, understanding and encouragement. If your child is constantly experiencing failure, their self-esteem can be badly affected. It is very important to find a way to help your child feel that success is possible and that you will help wherever you can.

A programme to develop motor skills competence

Children with dyspraxia can overcome their difficulties but they may need a structured and focussed exercise programme to do so. They need practice with activities in the following areas:

▲ Co-ordinated finger, hand and arm movements, for example turning a skipping rope, puzzles, games with shapes

▲ Hand-eye co-ordination, for example bean bags into a bucket, varied ball skills, playing chime bars with rhythm

▲ Foot-eye co-ordination, for example balancing on a line or beam, stepping stones, hopscotch, varied ball skills

▲ Balance, for example on separate legs, uneven surfaces balancing on a beam while carrying something, skateboard, bike

▲ Whole body co-ordination, for example crawling, tunnels, obstacle courses, running, climbing, swimming

▲ Sound, touch and movement, for example identify hidden objects by sound, touch, different hands, clapping rhythms

As children with dyspraxia often find their schoolwork very difficult, it is particularly important to help them persevere with regular practice on a daily basis. Parents should always make sure that the child finds these regular sessions enjoyable and can experience success.

41 Could my child have dyslexia, and how can I help?

The term dyslexia can be used whenever a child or adult encounters unexpected difficulties in learning to read, write or spell, in spite of being offered ordinary opportunities to learn within a classroom.

Children with dyslexia are not however all the same. The exact nature of their difficulties can vary. It is important to detect these difficulties in learning to read because children's self-esteem can be badly affected if they feel that in spite of their best efforts they are making no progress. It is particularly damaging if other people make the error of seeing the child as stupid or as not trying.

This leaflet looks at dyslexia in more depth and explains how you can help your child.

Some points to remember

▲ Every child with dyslexia is a little different.

▲ Children with dyslexia can usually be helped if their difficulties are recognised early enough and if they are given the right sort of support and encouragement in school and at home.

▲ If your child has reading and writing difficulties, have a think about whether they also have speech and language difficulties or any co-ordination difficulties. If they have speech and language difficulties it may be best to concentrate on helping them develop their speech and language skills, as a route to improving reading and writing. If they have some co-ordination difficulties you might wish to consider a wider assessment to include dyspraxia.

▲ Children with dyslexia find spelling extremely difficult. They often mix up letter order. They need extra structured support to learn the rules of spelling, and may take a lot longer to learn the early rules. Don't rush and don't criticise your child!

▲ Wherever possible, children with dyslexic difficulties should be taught to use joined up writing from the earliest possible age. Spelling should be taught via a focus on phonics and word families. The Schnoll spelling lists provide a useful framework.

▲ Children with reading and writing difficulties are often reluctant to keep trying. You can help your child by being firm about the need to keep practising and by persisting with *short* periods of daily practice in reading and writing skills at home. Make sure your child always experiences success.

▲ Always discuss your concerns with your child's school teachers. They will be able to offer additional advice and discuss with you whether a formal assessment might be of help.

What is dyslexia?

Dyslexia is best characterised as a disorder with a wide variety of symptoms and characteristics. Sometimes the difficulties are mild, sometimes they are more significant. The difficulties may include:

▲ Delays in speech and language development, notably difficulties with hesitant speech, in the awareness of sounds in words, and with remembering the names of things.

▲ Weak memory skills, particularly in the area of sounds

▲ Significant delays in learning to read

▲ Delays in developing clear handwriting

▲ Significant delays in learning to spell

▲ Delays in understanding maths and music.

Dyslexic children do not necessarily have all of these difficulties. Some dyslexia children have very good memory, language or maths skills. But children who experience dyslexia are born with the difficulty. It is more commonly found in boys than in girls and it is often found to run in families along with other language based difficulties. It is more commonly found in left-handed children.

What happens to the child with dyslexia?

The main difficulty for a child with dyslexic difficulties is that they do not make the easy progress with reading and writing that their peers do. This can be a source of great frustration to them and can switch them off school learning.

If you suspect that your child may be finding reading and writing really difficult it is *very* important to ask your school for a proper assessment and to give your child extra support, understanding and encouragement. If your child is constantly experiencing failure, his or her self-confidence can be badly affected. It is important to find a way to help your child feel that success is possible.

Helping your child with the language skills behind reading

In order to read and write effectively, children need to develop a good awareness of sounds in speech and then an awareness of the relationship between speech sounds, letters and words.

Activities to develop general speech skills include:

▲ As much direct turn-taking conversation as possible with adults who listen carefully, e.g. about the events of the day,

▲ Making up stories, taking messages and giving instructions

▲ Playing memory games such as 'I went to Market'.

Activities to develop sounds awareness include

▲ Singing and learning nursery rhymes and poems by heart

▲ Listening for rhymes

▲ Playing 'I Spy'

▲ Clapping out the syllables in longer words or sentences

▲ Learning the common letter groups that make key sounds in the English language.

Helping your child with reading and spelling

Research has found that dyslexic children learn best with structured step-by-step multisensory methods. This means that children need help to listen very carefully, to sound out and read word families, and to write words in a joined-up way so they can learn to feel the movements involved in common words.

Parents can help children with their difficulties by ensuring that the child does a small bit of reading and practice *on most days*. As the difficulties are very real, it is only by hard work and determination that they will be overcome. Parents can help the child overcome the tendency to wish to avoid this practice by making the sessions easy enough to always experience success, and enjoyable.

42 Obsessive–compulsive and repetitive behaviours, and how to help your child

Sometimes parents notice that their child appears to be obsessed with certain toys or routines or behaviours. It seems that the child cannot stop him or herself repeating certain actions. They become very tense or distressed if others try to prevent them carrying out the repetitive behaviour.

This leaflet looks at the nature of obsessive compulsive and repetitive behaviours and explains how you can help your child.

Some points to remember

▲ Young children often have a tendency to repeat the same behaviour or action or sound over and over again. In normal development these repetitive patterns are gradually replaced by more flexible behaviour.

▲ When much repetitive behaviour is seen in young children it may be a sign of some developmental delay. It is wise to ask for advice.

▲ If you think your child uses the behaviour as a form of self-stimulation it suggests that the world is hard to understand. The self-stimulation may be a way of escape or a habitual way of relaxing or self-soothing. Your child needs help learning to understand the world and building up alternative behaviours. This may take time.

▲ Obsessive-compulsive and repetitive behaviours often increase in intensity and frequency when a child is experiencing stress. Repeating the action has the effect of relieving some of the inner tension and makes them feel more relaxed. Can you help your child to talk about what is upsetting? And can you together think of some ways of relieving some of the pressure on your child.

▲ If you simply try to stop a child from carrying out an obsessive or repetitive behaviour he or she will often experience a huge build up or inner tension or anxiety. This tension may show with anxiety, anger or tantrums. It is therefore better to play things down and use distraction that helps the child develops alternative skills wherever possible.

▲ Older children with verbal skills can be helped to talk about the anxiety they experience when they are prevented from carrying out the repetitive actions. Talking openly about this anxiety and learning new ways of coping with it are important parts of effective treatments for these sorts of difficulties.

▲ Some repetitive behaviour can be eased by talking therapies or by medication. Do ask for professional advice if you are still worried.

What are obsessive–compulsive and repetitive behaviours?

Obsessive–compulsive and repetitive behaviours can be seen in many forms. For example:

- Small tics, stammers or jerky movements in parts of the body
- Repetitive speech or saying the same thing over and over again
- Repetitions of the same movement again and again
- Playing with toys in exactly the same way
- Carrying out routines in a particular and rigid way.
- Having strange thoughts or ideas that keep coming into one's head
- Repeatedly taking objects that belong to others.

A tendency to repetitive behaviours can run in families.

Obsessions and compulsions in young children

Many children have mild obsessions and compulsions at some time. In early development, infants love to repeat the same thing over and over again. This is the way they learn. They feel safe when they do things in the same way as then they can understand what is happening. These repetitive behaviour patterns are usually gradually replaced with more flexible and imaginative ways of behaving. So sometimes obsessive, compulsive and repetitive behaviour can be a sign that a child has developmental delay or learning difficulties

Obsessions and compulsions and stress

Obsessions and compulsions and repetitive behaviour often appear to increase in frequency and intensity when a person is under or has been under significant stress. If obsessive, compulsive and repetitive behaviour appears to be increasing, have a look at what might be upsetting your child at the present. Are there any steps you could take to relieve some pressure?

When are these behaviours a problem?

Mild levels of obsessive–compulsive and repetitive behaviours are surprisingly common and usually disappear over time. It is important for parents to keep an eye on their child but it does not help to draw too much attention to them. Making the child self-conscious or ashamed will just add to the child's inner tension and anxiety and probably make the problem worse. It is more important to find ways to help your child feel relaxed and happy and secure in his or her relationship with you and others.

Obsessive–compulsive and repetitive behaviours should be taken more seriously in the following circumstances:

- When they are taking up more than an hour of your child's day.
- When they are interfering with your child's ability to make relationships with others
- When they are causing distress to your child

Helping a child with repetitive behaviours

Repetitive behaviours can isolate a child from the normal social world. Sometimes the child finds the actions stimulating or soothing, sometimes it helps them avoid stressful situations, sometimes they are a direct communication. In all cases it is vital to try to understand your child's current experience and to find ways to increase your child's social skills and self-confidence.

If children have developed a long-standing habit of repetitive actions, they often do not like to be interrupted and may protest loudly to get you to leave them alone. But, while looking for ways to support and reduce pressure, it is wise to find ways to gently distract them onto a more useful and mentally flexible activity, preferably with other supportive people as much as possible.

43 Wetting and soiling, and how to help your child

Most children become dry and clean during the day in their second or third year with some occasional accidents. Most children stop needing nappies during their third or fourth year. Most become dry at night before the end of the fifth year.

So becoming dry and becoming clean are developmental issues. Some children are slower to acquire these skills than others. Sometimes however wetting and soiling appears to go on for longer than is expected. This can cause a lot of stress for the child within the family.

This leaflet will look at bedwetting and soiling in more depth and explain how you can help your child.

Some points to remember

▲ There are many different reasons for delays in becoming dry and clean. Each child will be different.

▲ A healthy gut and bladder are vital to healthy living. Mastering dryness and cleaness is very important to children's long–term well–being.

▲ It is helpful to let younger children see you enjoying using the toilet. Always be matter of fact. Use words that are comfortable in your family such as 'poo' and 'wee'. Toileting matters can be a bit smelly but try to avoid using words like 'disgusting'.

▲ Help your child learn to use the toilet at regular times of the day, for example just after breakfast, to establish some healthy habits that will support their long–term health. What is your child's natural rhythm? Provide some good books or magazines! Some children enjoy having a star chart to encourage them with their progress.

▲ If your child has any tendency to constipation, encourage them to look at their own poos/bowel movements and to start to notice if it is hard or soft. You can talk about what they need to eat and drink to keep it soft. Explain that hard poos/bowel movements can sometimes be a little painful.

▲ Bedwetting and soiling can start again in children who have been fully dry or clean. This commonly happens when children are upset or are coping with many big changes in their life such as when they start school or a new baby arrives or when there are arguments between parents.

▲ Very persistent wetting and soiling can sometimes be a symptom of significant emotional or physical stresses. How can you relieve some pressure?

▲ A very useful organisation that helps families is ERIC online (Education and Resources for Improving Childhood Continence). Always ask promptly for professional advice if you are still worried.

The development of dryness and cleanness

In normal development the control of wetting and soiling always develops gradually. Control of soiling usually comes first. Control of wetting is first gained in the day and later at night. Boys commonly have more problems with night wetting and girls with day wetting. To become dry and clean your child needs to develop the following:

▲ A regular bowel motion and regular needs to wee. *Make sure that your child has a balanced diet including plenty of fruit, vegetables, fibre and liquid.*

▲ Awareness of the sensations in her own body – in the bladder and in the bowel. *Encourage any signs of your child's acting on their awareness of their own needs. You can say 'I saw that you noticed you needed the toilet and you remembered to tell me/or you went all by yourself. Well done!'*

▲ Easy access to a toilet or potty and confidence in discussing the needs with you.

▲ Desire for and pleasure in the sensation and experience of dryness and cleanness as a sign of being more grown up. *You can say 'I can see that you have wiped yourself carefully, and your pants are all clean! Or your bed is all dry! Well done!' Or 'Let's put another star on your chart!*

▲ Confidence that you will not be cross about accidents. *You can say 'Never mind, it's just an accident. You can help me clean it up. I'm not cross. I'm pleased that you told me'.*

▲ Confidence that you care for them even though they have difficulties with this area. *Children are very sensitive to rejection. You can say: 'Some children find learning to be dry and clean harder than others. I am sure you will work it out one day. I still love you very much.'*

▲ Confidence that you are around and will listen to their worries. *Make some regular time to be around in a relaxed way. You can say, 'Some children wet the bed or soil when they are worried about things. If you'd like to talk to me, I will try to listen and help.'*

If your child is still not clean or dry, he or she may:

▲ *Just be a late developer.* He or she may just need more time. Be careful not to get cross as this will make the problem worse.

▲ *Have a tendency to rather weak control over the muscles in the bladder or gut.* Pay extra special attention to ensuring your child drinks enough liquid and eats enough fruit and vegetables and fibre through out the day and before going to bed. This strengthens the bladder muscles and prevents a build-up of over concentrated urine

▲ *Be worried about parents reactions.* Parents sometimes get too worried about little amounts of wee/urine and poo/soiling in pants. This can be counter-productive. Remember your child is learning a new skill. You can say 'Well done! That's hardly wet/dirty at all!'

▲ *Be experiencing emotional stresses or significant changes.* What pressures is your child under, how could you help?

▲ *Be experiencing painful or hard poos/faeces and bowel movements.* These can sometimes trigger fear of using the toilet and lead to a subsequent build up of constipation

▲ *Have a tendency to sleep very deeply and not wake up in response to needing to wee/urinate.*

▲ *Have an infection.* Wetting sometimes happens if a child has a urinary infection. This can be linked to insufficient fluids. Always seek early advice from your Doctor or Health Visitor.

▲ *Soiling sometimes occurs because a child has become seriously constipated.* Liquid faeces can begin to leak around the outside of a compacted area. Your child should have a poo/bowel movement most days. If they have gone 3 or more days without a poo/ bowel movement you should seek advice as soon as possible. Early intervention prevents long-term problems.

Some points to remember

▲ Your children will not all react in the same way. Their age, sex, temperament and the history of their own very personal relationships will influence the way each child reacts with each parent.

▲ In the period before, during and after separation and divorce adults and children feel many mixed and confusing emotions. Children need support in acknowledging these emotions. It is helpful for a child to know that the parents feel a range of emotions too but it is not helpful to burden the child with responsibility for the parent's emotions.

▲ Parents can help children by giving them an opportunity to express their views and feelings about what is happening and about their wishes. But parents should make sure that the child understands that the responsibility for the break up is theirs and only theirs. Children should never be made to feel to blame.

▲ Wherever possible, children need to know that they still have two parents who love them and will continue to care for them whatever happens. Children need to continue to have reliable ordinary time with both of their parents on ordinary things.

▲ As far as possible try to keep as much stability in other aspects of the child's life so that other relationships with peers and wider family members are not also affected.

▲ Aim, wherever possible, to restore an amicable relationship with your ex-partner in the long-run. This will help your child enormously.

▲ Don't hesitate to seek professional support if you are worried.

---

44 Helping children cope with separation and divorce

If you are currently considering separation or divorce or if this has recently happened for you, this is probably a difficult time for you. If you have children you may be wondering about how they will be affected and about what you can do to help. The separation or divorce of their parents always affects children as it turns their world upside down, but this painful situation can be made more or less difficult by the details of the way in which it is handled.

This leaflet will look at how separation and divorce affects children and will explain how you can help your child.

The effect of arguments, aggression and violence between parents

Although they may not always show it, children are very upset when they see one of their parents abusing, shouting at or attacking the other one.

Younger children may become anxious; complain of tummy aches, or start to wet the bed. They may find it difficult to sleep, have more tantrums or regress in their behaviour to a younger age

Older children react differently. Girls are more likely to keep their distress inside. They may become moody, argumentative, anxious or depressed. They may complain of vague physical symptoms, develop an eating disorder or show signs of self-harm. Boys may become more withdrawn or more aggressive and disobedient, using violence themselves to deal with problems. School performance is commonly affected as children find it difficult to concentrate on their studies.

The effect of these family situations on children is worse if they are targets of aggression themselves, if their general care is neglected, or if they are involved in taking sides in the disputes.

The impact of separation and divorce on children

When parents decide that they can no longer live together, the child's world changes for ever. Sometimes if there has been a lot of arguing and fighting, the separation may bring some welcome relief. If it comes out of the blue, children may simply not understand what has happened. In both cases however, the child has to cope with many different and conflicting emotions including anger, sadness, anxiety, guilt and longing. Most children just want an ordinary stable and loving family to grow up in.

Understanding some of the complex emotions

Children's emotions about the separation and/or divorce of their parents are usually very complex. Here are some examples of what they may feel:

- ▲ Relief that the fighting has or might be stopping
- ▲ Anxious that the separation was their fault
- ▲ Torn in two by loyalty to both parents
- ▲ Abandoned and rejected by the parent who has left
- ▲ Anxious that the other parent might abandon them too
- ▲ Angry with one or both parents for their failures
- ▲ Sad that they can't express their love for the other parent
- ▲ Confused about why it happened
- ▲ Lonely because there is less contact with adults now
- ▲ Resentful at the loss of other opportunities
- ▲ Worried about their own future in relationships
- ▲ Protective of the most distressed parent.

Loving and hating is very mixed up together in a child's experience of their parent's divorce. These confused emotions often lead to confusing and unpredictable behaviour.

Helping your child

Because your child's emotions will be so conflicted, he or she will need a lot of patient understanding and support from you over a long period of time. It helps to keep ordinary things going and the channels of communication open. Wherever possible, work towards a more amicable relationship with your ex-partner, even if this takes some years to achieve. This will help you but it will also help your child have faith in the fact that though relationships can be difficult, forgiveness and understanding is possible and worth working for.

45

Helping children cope with death and loss

In every person's life, there comes a point when they must face the reality of death. For children this commonly first happens in the context of the death of an elderly grandparent or a pet.

But sometimes children have to cope with death in the context of more traumatic circumstances, such as is the case in the death of a parent, a sibling or a friend as a result of illness or an accident.

Parents and carers often have very strong feelings of their own in these circumstances and may feel confused about how to best help their children.

This leaflet gives some ideas about how to help your child.

Some points to remember

▲ People will react in different ways to the death of someone special. These differences come from differences in their personality, differences in their age and differences in the nature of their relationship to the person who has died.

▲ Children and adults need *time* to adjust to someone's death. The process of adjustment can take months and sometimes years. It is not helpful to expect grieving to be suddenly over.

▲ Always take into account your child's developmental age. Death of someone important can be particularly unsettling for children. It can make their world feel very unsafe.

▲ Wherever possible it is helpful to involve children in ways that will help them understand that something important and final has happened, and that other people also feel sad and upset about it. Attending a funeral can be an important way of coming to an understanding of death.

▲ Do try to keep talking about the person who has died with your child. Talk about the precious happy memories that you have.Look at photographs together and go to special places.

▲ Don't be afraid to talk about times when that person made you cross or upset. Sometimes children find it very hard to feel cross with someone who died. It will help them if they know you feel these feelings too.

▲ During the period of adjustment try to keep as many of the other aspects of your child's life as similar as possible. Remember, stresses accumulate. Your child is more likely to struggle if there are many changes close together.

▲ Do ask for professional support if you are still worried.

The feelings when someone dies

When someone special dies, children and adults can feel a range of emotions. These include:

▲ Shock and numbness
▲ Anxiety and insecurity
▲ Guilt
▲ Protest and anger
▲ Sadness and depression.

Exactly which emotions a person feels, and the intensity with which they feel them varies considerably, according to the circumstances of the death and to the age of the child.

The impact of a child's age

Children will make sense of the death of someone in relation to what they already understand about the world. The nature of their grief will be strongly affected by the quality of their own relationship with the person who has died. Young babies will be affected by the loss of a principal carer, but may also respond to the feelings of sadness and tension in other members of the family who are themselves struggling with grief. They may seem more irritable and difficult to settle.

Pre-school and infant children can believe that death is reversible and that the person will come back again. But during the primary school years most children come to understand that death involves a permanent separation. Young children are apt to believe that they caused the death, for example by being naughty. They may not appear sad. But aspects of their behaviour may change. Teenagers often find it difficult to put feelings into words. It is important to watch their behaviour for clues as to how they are feeling and coping.

Helping children to cope with death

Adults are often not sure about how to help children cope with death and want to protect them from pain. However we now know that wherever possible it is better to be honest with children and let them participate from the beginning in the process of adjusting to a loved person's death.

▲ Tell your child as soon as possible about what has happened.

▲ In a gentle way, explain to them the details of what has happened and why. Let them ask questions and answer them to the best of your ability.

▲ Reassure your child that there are still people around who will be able to care for him or her.

▲ Let them see the dead person or pet or attend the funeral if possible, especially if they were close to that person. Help them find a way to say goodbye.

▲ Acknowledge that your child may have some very strong and mixed feelings about the death. Let them know that it may take some time for everyone to feel less sad and upset

▲ Remember to continue talking about happy memories of the person who has died, looking at photos and visiting special places

When to seek more help

Given the right support most children do adjust to the loss of a loved person. Sometimes though the process is not quite so smooth It is appropriate to seek help if:

▲ Your child falls into a more serious depression
▲ He or she seems excessively anxious,
▲ He or she continually denies that the death has happened
▲ They frequently talk about wanting to join the dead person.

46 Helping children cope with trauma

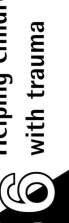

Sometimes in spite of parent's best efforts, children are exposed to traumatic or upsetting experiences. Parents are often as upset about what has happened as their child. Sometimes parents are not sure whether the child is 'traumatised' or not. In both cases parents can feel confused about what they can best do to help their child

This leaflet looks at the nature of trauma and its effects in more depth and explains how you can help yourself and your child.

Some points to remember

▲ Remember traumatic events happen to many people. They are hard to deal with at the time but if they are dealt with in a positive and supportive way your child will probably have more understanding and more skills to use in relation to future events.

▲ It is helpful to talk with your child in a matter of fact way about the event and about the different feelings that each person had. You might say for example: *'I guess you must have felt very frightened. Perhaps you wondered why I wasn't there to help you'.*

▲ If you create an open matter of fact style then your child may talk about it with you at unexpected times. Remember that processing traumatic events takes time. It can sometimes take years. The trauma is rarely forgotten completely.

▲ Some children find it difficult to talk about their feelings but you can sense that they are still bothered by their behaviour and their play. Watch carefully and try to understand what your child may be feeling. Many trauma reactions are about feeling unsafe and/or angry with others that can't be trusted.

▲ Try to keep a positive focus and keep other things stable. Your child needs time to work things out but also needs to have good things to enjoy and look forward to in their future.

▲ If you are struggling with your own emotions, it is important to try to find someone to help you talk them through. Don't ask your child to help you. This is not their responsibility.

▲ If you are sure your child is struggling and you feel unable to help do ask for professional help, advice and support.

What sorts of experiences are 'traumatic'?

Trauma reactions are normally found after situations in which a person has felt extremely frightened because the things that were happening to them were terrifying and seemed to be seriously out of control. The person felt there was nothing that they could do to stop the terrifying events that were taking place to them or around them.

Traumatic experiences can happen to individuals. They include things such as car crashes, house fires, domestic violence, domestic crime and emotional, physical and sexual abuse, and prolonged separation experiences in infancy. Trauma can also affect whole communities following events such as earthquakes, floods and war.

One of the key elements that determines whether a person experiences long-term trauma effects is whether they felt at the time that there were other reliable people that they could turn to for assistance.

What are the symptoms of Post-Traumatic Stress Disorder?

Following a trauma experience there are some common reactions:

▲ *Numbness and no feeling* (in some people this numbness or blocking and avoidance of thoughts of the events can last a long time)
▲ *Anxiety and preoccupation with the event* (including flash-backs, sleeplessness and difficulties concentrating)
▲ *Guilt, protest and anger* (often about survival or what was not done and/or about what others didn't do)
▲ *Depression and sadness* (often about the consequences of the event and the fact that they can't be changed).

Individual reactions vary according to the specific details of the event, the person's age and temperament and previous experiences.

The cumulative effects of trauma

People often wonder why trauma experiences affect some people so much and not others. And why is it that trauma reactions seem to sometimes appear so much after the initial event?

Infants and adults have coping mechanisms that help them to cope with ordinary levels of stressful events. One of the most important ways of coping is to move on and not to think too much about what happened. Blocking out stressful and painful feelings and memories can, and does, help people to function in their everyday life.

However, sometimes the way of coping that involves not thinking and not talking about feelings or past experiences, starts to be no longer effective because there are other new stresses that are pushing this method of coping to the limit. All of a sudden people can find themselves overwhelmed by distressing thoughts and feelings that are hard to understand because their intensity is greater than current events would seem to justify.

There is now quite a lot of evidence to suggest that children who were exposed to early trauma or early stressful events are more vulnerable to stronger reactions if they experience other traumas or significant stresses later in life.

Helping your child

If you feel your child has been exposed to a trauma you need to take it seriously, but you must also strike an important balance. It is important to talk about what happened so that the child can make sense of it and can know that it wasn't their fault and that these things don't happen often. But it is also important to help the child get on in a positive way with things in their normal life. It is very unhelpful to give a child the message that they will never be normal again.

Helping children with bullying and teasing

Lots of people have fun with ordinary gentle teasing. In fact we often use gentle teasing when we feel some affection for another person. We find something that gets a slight reaction from them and what we say makes everyone laugh a bit. When it is the nice ordinary teasing, the teased person can see the funny side too.

In contrast, bullying is a nasty sort of teasing linked with some sort of physical or emotional threat or intimidation that makes the other person feel upset, frightened or unhappy.

This leaflet explains about teasing and bullying and about how you can help your child.

Ways of helping children stop bullying or nasty teasing

Improve your child's self-esteem and self-confidence
Schools and the work place are challenging places for children. Your child will be less likely to become a bully, and will be more resistant to bullying and teasing if they are confident about themselves. There are lots of ideas about how to do this on the leaflet entitled, 'Building your child's self-esteem and self-confidence'.

Help your child learn to shrug off teasing
Sensitive children are often more vulnerable to bullying. But you can help a sensitive child by:

▲ Talking with them about the things he/she gets teased about

▲ Showing sympathy for how difficult it must be

▲ Practising some methods of responding, for example:
　– I'm not ashamed of wearing glasses
　– Staying calm, counting to 10
　– Ignoring, walking away
　– Finding a friend or a teacher

▲ Helping your child work out methods of avoiding bullies

▲ Helping your child build up a network of supportive friends

▲ Encouraging your child to talk about their successes in coping.

Talk to others yourself
If you are still concerned:

▲ Talk to other parents to find out if they are worried

▲ Talk to your child's teacher or head-teacher

▲ Talk to the child's parent in a calm but firm way.

Signs and symptoms of bullying or nasty teasing

Children don't find it easy to tell adults that they are being teased or bullied. They may be afraid that it will make things worse. Parents need to be alert to some tell-tale signs such as:

- Unexplained withdrawn behaviour
- Unexplained bouts of crying or irritability
- Anxiety or reluctance about going to certain places
- Loss of self-confidence or increased sensitivity
- Change in sleep patterns or appetite
- Reluctance to talk
- Unexplained damage to or loss of possessions
- Unexplained injuries or bruises.

Why do some people become bullies?

- Bullies have often been a victim of persistent bullying themselves in another setting. Bullying others gives them an outlet for the feelings of anger and powerlessness they feel or have felt in other settings.
- Bullies may have experienced others using hostile, harsh or aggressive methods to sort out problems. When children see a lot of aggression they think it is normal and that it pays.
- Bullies may be struggling with feelings of jealousy or insecurity in relation to others. They make themselves feel better or stronger by picking on someone weaker.
- Bullies may be trying to be popular with friends by showing that they can be tough and hard. The way adults react can make a difference.

Why are some people teased and bullied a lot?

- Bullies often pick on someone who seems different in some way
- Bullies are more likely to pick on someone who is sensitive, who gets upset or angry very quickly
- Bullies often pick on people with low self-confidence who finds it hard to stand up for themselves.
- Bullies will carry on unless they are stopped.

First steps, if you suspect the presence of nasty teasing and bullying

If you discover that your child is being a bully or is being bullied there are a number of things you can do:

- Don't act too hastily. Monitor the situation carefully.
- Listen carefully to your child. What does your child think would be helpful?
- Ask yourself about the teasing and bullying that goes on in your own home. What does your child experience? How does it help your child in other settings?
- Is it possible that your child has low self-esteem or low self-confidence? Are their things that you could do to help?

48 My child may have some special education needs – what should I do?

If your child has difficulties of any sort (with learning, movement, speech, toileting or behaviour) it is important to think about whether they may need special consideration or help in school or in nursery.

There are some clear rules that explain what parents and professionals need to do in order to request extra help for a child in school or nursery. The rules also determine which children get extra help and what sort of help they can get.

This leaflet tries to explain what the rules are and what you can do to help your child.

Some points to remember

▲ The UK Government now has an active policy of trying to provide for most children with special educational needs within mainstream settings in their own local communities.

▲ Professionals are required by law to notify the LEA at the earliest possible date, if they have any reason to believe that a child may have some special educational needs. This helps the LEA to begin its planning process.

▲ When the LEA is asked to consider carrying out a statutory assessment of your child's SSEN, it must reply to the request within six weeks. Remember, the LEA is more likely to refuse if it was sent very limited information at an early stage.

▲ The LEA should provide you with full information about the process and the time limits involved. Remember, carrying out an assessment is not the same as agreeing to a Statement. The evidence that you can provide at every stage is critical.

▲ The LEA should give you the name of a local independent Parent Partnership scheme. These organisations are set up to support families.

▲ If your child is not toilet-trained or if he or she has any significant health or movement difficulties, he or she will not be able to attend a mainstream setting without support. If you have concerns speak to your health visitor or to the school in good time.

▲ Parental views are very important, and parents have important rights under the Special Education Act, which gives them the right of appeal to the SEN Tribunal. Wherever possible, parents hare encouraged to work in co-operation with the schools and with the LEA, and to use other means of disagreement resolution.

▲ Meeting a child's SEN requires determination as well as good will and teamwork from many parties. To support your child you will need to be very assertive and firm. But don't alienate those who can support you!

Requests to the local education authority (LEA) for a statutory assessment

▲ Parents, teacher and SENCO believe that child's needs cannot be catered for under Action or Action Plus.

▲ Parents and professionals have to *consider* whether a statutory multidisciplinary assessment of the child's educational needs is appropriate. They can request that the LEA consider a statement.

▲ If they believe a lot of extra help is needed, parents and professionals must provide detailed evidence about the child's difficulties from people who know the child. This evidence must indicate why the child's needs cannot be met within standard mainstream provision.

▲ If the local education authority agrees that there is enough evidence of a need for a statutory assessment, it will ask its own educational psychologists to carry out an assessment and will formally approach any professional who already knows the child for their views, including:

　– A medical report
　– A report from an educational setting the child has attended
　– Advice from professionals with expertise in the child's area of difficulty, especially if equipment or lifting will be required
　– Parental views (and those of the child if possible).

▲ The outcome of the statutory assessment process may or may not be a **Statement of Special Educational Needs (SEN)**. The statement is a legal document that should specify in detail what extra help will be provided for the child.

A statutory assessment is likely to be appropriate if the child is thought to need very high levels of special support. Parents should be aware however that most Education Authorities are now trying to provide for the majority of children under Action and Action Plus. Statements are obtained by less than two per cent of all children.

What help is available?

Though many children have some degree of special educational needs, it is very difficult to get additional funding for an individual child's special educational needs. Very few children indeed get additional one to one help in school and very few of these get one to one help from a qualified teacher.

Help is usually provided for a group of children with special needs and it is usually provided by a SSA (Special Support Assistant) who will be working under the direction of a teacher.

However, all schools are now required to have a Special Educational Needs Co-ordinator (a SENCO) and a Register of children with special needs. And, all teachers are required to see themselves as teachers of children with special educational needs. This means that every teacher must identify children in their own class who are having difficulties and must assess the level of their needs according to the following criteria:

Special Needs Action

▲ Teacher, parents and SENCO agree on cause for concern

▲ Individual Educational Plan (IEP) written for child, with three or four targets specifically related to the child's needs

▲ IEP reviewed regularly

▲ School has no additional support or funding

Special Needs Action Plus

▲ Teacher, parents and SENCO agree that child's needs cannot be met within school's own resources

▲ School develops IEP applies for support from other agencies

▲ School seeks funding for special support assistants according to a clear *local* formula. For example:

　– One child in class – two hours SSA per session
　– Two children in class – two and a half hours SSA per session.

49 Supporting children with writing

Teachers who work with primary age children base their teaching on a structured set of curriculum tools. This allows them to assess your child's progress, and to identify the difficulties they are having. Children and parents do not always know what these assessments are looking at.

This leaflet attempts to give *you* an idea of the some of the different areas of skill in writing that are commonly developed. Children can use it to think about their own work and next steps. Or if your child is having difficulty, it may give you some ideas of how to support him or her so that they do not lose confidence.

To use the chart: i) Work out what your child currently finds easy, ii) Are there any particular areas in which your child is having difficulties? iii) Talk to your child about the areas which are assessed and about the things that teachers look for, iv) Provide more opportunities to help them practice and develop their existing skills, iv) *Don't* be tempted to rush your child on before he/she is ready.

Some points to remember

▲ It is not easy to compare different school systems exactly. However, in both the English and Scottish systems, each level commonly takes one to two years to complete. The majority of 7 year olds achieve a level B or a 2, the majority of 11 year olds achieve a level D or 4. Some children progress through the levels more slowly, some progress more quickly

▲ You cannot build a house without good foundations. Don't ever be tempted to rush your child.

▲ The majority of children enjoy school work if they are encouraged at home and at school and feel that they understand and can achieve regular success.

▲ If your child is not confident on some of the early skills it is much better to go back to some very simple exercises and develop your child's confidence in the basic steps before working at a harder level. Regular short periods of daily practice are most effective.

▲ Some children who have difficulties with writing need a lot more practice with reading and speaking. Regular reading aloud helps children with spelling and with sentence structure. Regular practice in conversation helps children develop confidence in putting their ideas into words.

▲ A few children who have difficulties with writing have a condition known as 'dyslexia.' Early assessment and diagnosis of dyslexia is vital. But dyslexic difficulties can only be overcome with careful teaching and much perseverance.

▲ If you have concerns about your child's progress, wherever possible make a point of building a good relationship with your child's teacher so that you can work with them to help build your child's confidence.

Criteria for Assessing Extended Writing Skills*

	Stage 1 – A	Stage 2 – B	Stage 3 – C	Stage 4 – D	Stage 5 – E
Volume possible in 30–40 mins of concentration (after discussion/ planning)	6/7 lines	1/2 A4 page	3/4 A4 page	1 A4 page+	1 A4 page+
Presentation/Handwriting	Most letters formed correctly Clear title	Letters correctly formed Some words joined Even size of letters	Most words joined Most sentences even Care on layout	Mature joined style Mostly even and consistent Careful clean layout	Attractive setting out of page
Choice and use of language	Writing includes what happened or events	Writing includes: – People involved – What happened or events – One or two interesting adjectives – One or two specific verbs, for example 'The fierce dog growled'.	Writing includes: – Places or settings – People and feelings – What happened/events – Several interesting verbs, adjectives and adverbs, expressions	Writing is rich with details: – Detail of places – Characters and feelings – What happened or events – Frequent use interesting words and expressions – We want to read more	The language and detail create a very accurate and convincing picture of characters, atmosphere, and events
Spelling	Schonell Group 1 Core word list	Schonell Group 2 Most regular phonic-based words	Schonell Group 3 Less common words spelled with phonic rules	Schonell Group 4 Uses a few more challenging words	Schonell Group 5 Uses quite a lot of sophisticated words
Selection and organisation of ideas	At least two or three different details Some simple link words, for example and, then	Details make a sequence of events clear Details are beginning to be organised, for example with beginning, middle and end Links: but, so, that	Writer establishes a setting or context at start Details help reader make sense of events No big gaps or repetition Varied sentence structure At least 1 paragraph	Sets a clear context or setting for events or feeling Account is rounded off or somehow concluded Varied sentences Several paragraphs each containing different ideas or events A personal style shows	Clear setting for events or feelings Account has an overall shape, with a turning point or climax Sentences of different lengths and types Accurate use of paragraphs for ideas, etc
Punctuation and meaning	At least one sentence with a capital letter and full stop At least one use of capital for proper name	More than one sentence accurate with capitals, stop Mainly consistent use of tense Sentences mainly have no words missing More than one proper name with capital At least one adjective and adverb	Most sentences are accurately punctuated More than one example of commas, speech, questions Mostly clear and accurate meanings, including use of tense Mainly accurate use of capitals for proper names Several adjectives and adverbs	Full range of punctuation used most of the time Confident use of additional punctuation including speech, commas Consistent use of tenses throughout writing Clear complete sentences Confidence with capitals	Punctuation accurately and reliably supports the structure and meaning of the writing

*This is a guide only based loosely on the English and Scottish assessment systems.

Teachers who work with primary age children base their teaching on a structured set of curriculum tools. This allows them to support your child's progress, and to identify the difficulties they are having. Unfortunately, children and parents do not always know what these assessments are based on.

This leaflet attempts to give you, an idea of the some of the different areas of skill in maths that are commonly taught and assessed. If your child is having difficulty it is important to support them so that they do not lose confidence.

To use the chart: i) Work out what your child currently finds easy, ii) Are there any particular areas your child finds difficult?, iii) Talk to your child about the areas which are assessed and about the things that teachers look for, iv) Provide more opportunities to help them practice and develop their existing skills, iv) *Don't* be tempted to rush your child on before he/she is ready.

Some points to remember

▲ It is not easy to compare different school systems exactly. However, in both the English and Scottish systems, each level commonly takes one to two years to complete. The majority of 7 year olds achieve a level B or a 2; most 11 year olds achieve a level D or a 4.

▲ The modern approach to maths teaching focuses on teaching a range of strategies for solving problems and on confidence in using numbers rather than on teaching one method of answering sums.

▲ Some children progress through the levels more slowly, some progress more quickly. But you cannot build a house without good foundations. Don't ever be tempted to rush your child.

▲ The majority of children enjoy school work if they are encouraged at home and at school and feel that they understand and can achieve regular success.

▲ If your child is not confident on some of the early skills it is much better to go back to some very simple exercises and develop your child's confidence in the basic steps before working at a harder level. Regular short periods of daily practice (10–15mins) are most effective.

▲ Many of the children who have difficulties with maths simply need a lot more practice with basic number bonds. That is practice with the ways that 3 numbers can be linked using addition and subtraction, and other sets of 3 numbers can be linked with multiplying and dividing (see over). Regular practice with simple number bonds and tables, so knowledge of the relationships becomes automatic, provides an essential foundation for ease with more complex calculations.

▲ A few children who have difficulties with maths have a condition known as dyscalculia. Early assessment and diagnosis of dyscalculia is vital. However, dyscalculic difficulties can only be overcome with careful teaching and much perseverance.

▲ If you have concerns about your child's progress, wherever possible make a point of building a good relationship with your child's teacher so that you can work with them to help build your child's confidence.

Criteria for Assessing Maths and Numeracy Skills*

	Stage 1 – A	Stage 2 – B	Stage 3 – C	Stage 4 – D	Stage 5 – E
Place value	0–10 The number line Tens and units	0–100 The hundred square Hundreds, tens, units	Two- to three-digit number sums Decimal point	0–10,000	0–1,000,000
Adding and subtracting Note four bonds $6 + 4 = 10, 4 + 6 = 10$ $10 - 4 = 6, 10 - 6 = 4$	Number bonds to 10 Counting on Counting back Making up the difference $(3 + \ldots = 10)$ Simple word problems	Number bonds to 100 Two-digit adding – no carrying Two-digit subtracting, no decomposition Adding 9 or 19 Taking away 9 or 19	All bonds confident Adding with carrying Adding decimals Subtracting with decomposition Word problems	Adding and subtracting using hundreds and thousands Agility with larger numbers	Agility with larger numbers More complex word problems
Multiplying and dividing Note four bonds: $6 \times 3 = 18, 3 \times 6 = 18$ $18 \div 3 = 6, 18 \div 6 = 3$	2x, 5x, 10x Doubling and halving	The notion of multiplication as repeated addition 2x, 3x, 4x, 5x, 10x Simple divides Patterns in numbers	All tables confident Multiply/divide by 100 Multiplying two digits by one digit Divide with remainder	Multiples of tables eg x40 and x400 Multiplying two digits by two digits Dividing three digits by one digit	Multiplying three digits by two digits Dividing three or four digits by two or three digits
Money	Pence up to 50p	Pence up to 100p	Pounds and pence	Larger more complex amounts	More complex word problems
Estimating and Measuring	Whole metres, cm Using a ruler	Non-standard units (eg handspans)	Kg and Litres Millimetres, millilitres Reading scales	Number problems using different measures	Two-step calculations using distance, weight and volume
Time	Seasons, months problems Days of week Hours and o'clock	Half-past, quarters Digital format	Ten past, 20 past, etc Simple time calculations am and pm	24-hour clock Timetables	Complex calculations and word 24-hour calculations
Shape	Simple 2D shapes: square, circle, triangle	Simple properties 3D sphere, cuboid, etc One-line symmetry	Complex properties: right angles, two lines symmetry Calculating perimeter	Area Right angles	Calculating volume of 3D shapes Acute, obtuse angles Rotational symmetry Use of a compass
Fractions/decimals	Half of shapes	Halves and quarters Half of a number	Three-quarters 50%	Fifths, sixths, tenths Fractions of numbers 10% 25% 75%	Complex fractions and decimal Equivalence 50% = ½ = 0.5
Tables and graphs	Reading a table	Block graphs	Line graphs Tally charts	Extracting and organising information and drawing graphs	Reading and constructing complex tables and graphs

*This is a guide only based loosely on the English and Scottish assessment systems.

51 Becoming a parent of a child with a disability

No one can prepare for the adjustments involved in becoming a parent of a child with a disability.

In this leaflet, four parents share their experiences of what life has been like for them.

A very useful UK-based organisation for parents, particularly those whose children have rarer conditions, is 'Contact A Family'. This group provides a huge amount of information to help families to meet others who have been through similar experiences.

Most countries and states will have similar groups that can be contacted for help and support.

It's sort of like a survival course, you have to learn such a lot because you're suddenly put in a situation where you only have yourself to rely on and most of your past experience isn't much help, because this is something entirely new and different and frightening.

So you need to learn lots quickly like how to cope with strong and perhaps negative emotions; who you can talk to; where you can find them; how to keep going despite sheer exhaustion; who to ask for practical help; how to find out what's available.

Of course, it might take some time even before the questions become clear, but that time passes and I remember it as a haze, something like childbirth, it's bad at the time but you can't remember it properly afterwards so it becomes okay. From then on it is as if you have your own education course and the more you put in the more you get out, and the more you can give to others down the line.

I think that life with my son who is different and yet the same is just like that, the emotions are exactly the same as I feel towards my other child, but they are different because everything is exaggerated, there's more pain when I know he is lonely or upset or frustrated, but also when he achieves, the pride is enormous, when he's happy the joy in his happiness is so great and when he achieves, which usually takes more time and effort than other people use in a year; wow!

Anonymous

I never thought it would be this hard. 'She's got cerebral palsy', they said. 'What exactly is that?' I thought. I was determined to find out what this meant: Endless reading up, expecting answers all the time, but never getting enough. I realise now that there are none.

I felt my world had collapsed. How could I come to terms with this? But you do. Of course I didn't believe them at first. But slowly the truth shows.

I think I have gone through every emotion and then another one turns up. My life has changed so much and I feel I am a different person. But this was not through choice and it wouldn't have been so hard to take if it had been that way. However, so be it and you carry on regardless. You make the best out of a situation and hope springs eternal. If you don't have faith, then you have nothing.

Support networks are a godsend and having someone to talk to who understands and who has been through something similar helps. I feel I am coping quite well at the moment, but every day, week, month can be different.

I know I am a stronger person but hope I have the strength to stay the course before cracking under the strain. I worry all the time, for now, for the future, but her determination is encouraging, extremely tiring but still encouraging...

Anonymous

What is a bombshell? Being told your first child is going to have a severe learning disability, the day after she was born. Then the fun starts, and the fight. Yes, you have to fight all the time for your rights. Which benefits and schooling, what the future holds.

At every hurdle, you feel another blow, always striving for positive outcomes. Support is always promised but is very rarely forthcoming. Nothing comes to those who don't ASK, ASK and keep on asking.

Always planning for the future, who will care for my daughter when we are gone?

Anonymous

When I recall those days after the diagnosis, I can only remember the suffering and the tears and the horror. How many nights had I had been crying and accusing God and myself for such a curse? How many times did I ask God what I had done for my sweet child to be so totally different? I thought what a relief it would be if he was never born or something just happened to him. Then I blamed myself for such thoughts. I felt so guilty for everything, so miserable and unhappy ...

But we have changed so much. We now know what it is to love unconditionally. We embrace ourselves instead of fighting. We talk to each other and to our kids instead of yelling. We respect ourselves and others. We accept ourselves and others. We are the parents we always wanted to be but we didn't know how. We are friends to each other and to the world ...

Anonymous